WALKING SYDNEY

BELINDA CASTLES is the award-winning author of four novels, *Bluebottle*, *Hannah and Emil*, *The River Baptists* and *Falling Woman*, and editor of the collection *Reading Like an Australian Writer*. She teaches writing at the University of Sydney.

WALKING SYDNEY

FIFTEEN WALKS WITH A CITY'S WRITERS

BELINDA CASTLES

NEWSOUTH

UNSW Press acknowledges the Bedegal people, the Traditional Owners of the unceded territory on which the Randwick and Kensington campuses of UNSW are situated, and recognises the continuing connection to Country and culture. We pay our respects to Bedegal Elders past and present.

A NewSouth book

Published by
NewSouth Publishing
University of New South Wales Press Ltd
University of New South Wales
Sydney NSW 2052
AUSTRALIA
https://unsw.press/

Our authorised representative in the EU for product safety is Mare Nostrum Group B.V., Mauritskade 21D, 1091 GC Amsterdam, The Netherlands (gpsr@mare-nostrum.co.uk).

© Belinda Castles 2025
First published 2025

This book is copyright. Apart from any fair dealing for the purpose of private study, research, criticism or review, as permitted under the *Copyright Act*, no part of this book may be reproduced by any process without written permission. Inquiries should be addressed to the publisher.

 A catalogue record for this book is available from the National Library of Australia

ISBN   9781742237930 (paperback)
           9781761179310 (ebook)
           9781761178573 (ePDF)

Cover design and illustrations Mika Tabata
Internal design Josephine Pajor-Markus

All reasonable efforts were taken to obtain permission to use copyright material reproduced in this book, but in some cases copyright could not be traced. The author welcomes information in this regard.

These walks and the writing of this book took place on the lands of the Gadigal, Bidjigal, Birrabirragal, Burramattagal, Dharawal, Cabrogal, Cammeraygal and Garigal peoples. The stories of the area now known as Sydney go back tens of thousands of years. This place always was and always will be Aboriginal land.

CONTENTS

INTRODUCTION
Reading Sydney   1

YINDYAMARRA
Eveleigh and Carriageworks with Jazz Money   13

HISTORY BENEATH YOUR FEET
Surry Hills with Fiona Kelly McGregor   27

VERTICALS OF LIGHT
The Rocks, Walsh Bay and Circular Quay
with Gail Jones   43

PARRAMATTA WILL NEVER BE COMPLETE
Parramatta with Eda Gunaydin   59

SLIPPING INTO THE CURRENT
King Street, Newtown with Vanessa Berry   75

THE IDEA OF A BEACH
Freshwater with Malcolm Knox   91

TODAY
Yagoona and Bankstown with Sheila Ngọc Phạm   103

TIDAL CITY
Rushcutters Bay Park and Elizabeth Bay with
Delia Falconer   121

WALKING ON CAMMERAYGAL COUNTRY
North Willoughby and Middle Cove with Jakelin Troy   137

SOME SECRET TO LIFE
Casula and Liverpool with Max Easton   151

A MAGIC TO THE MIRE
   Kings Cross, Darlinghurst and Surry Hills
   with Neal Drinnan   165

FEEL EACH PART OF YOUR FOOT ON THE GROUND
   Bronte and Clovelly with Beth Yahp   179

CREATING A LIBRARY
   Bankstown and Punchbowl Boys' High School
   with Michael Mohammed Ahmad   193

A PLACE OF REVELATIONS
   Cooks River with Michelle de Kretser   207

ALWAYS HERE
   City and Redfern with Larissa Behrendt   219

AFTERWORD
   The city is alive   237

NOTES   241

ABOUT THE WALKERS   255

ACKNOWLEDGEMENTS   261

There are many versions of Sydney. The architectural miscellany of the central city; the postcolonial city with the legacy of Indigenous dispossession; the party city of Mardi Gras and fireworks; the sprawling suburban network of traffic snarls and local enclaves. Sydney is all and more of these at once. Its landscapes hold the memories of everyone whose lives have taken place here, the imprints of past times and future dreams.

– Vanessa Berry, *Mirror Sydney*

Parisian writers always gave the street address of their characters, as though all readers knew Paris so well that only a real location in the streets would breathe life into a character, as though histories and stories themselves had taken up residence throughout the city.

– Rebecca Solnit, *Wanderlust*

Spellings of names for Aboriginal places, peoples and objects vary according to preferences and source texts.

INTRODUCTION – READING SYDNEY

There is a rust-coloured beach in northern Sydney where I have long walked in the evenings. Ferns and scrub and a little waterfall spill down the sandstone headland. Houses teeter on the cliff. In the last soft light, I wander along the cool sand, and the mysteries of houses and other people beckon as the shapes of the world become indistinct.

From my early days in Sydney, my walks have carried the strangeness of encounter; I travel ever further into the labyrinth to see what I will find. Heading out from my first Sydney home, a condemned studio in Elizabeth Bay, I walked steep staircases and hills, passing continually from shadow into the dazzle of light on water. In Chippendale and Newtown I breathed petrol fumes and jasmine among terraces and curious old factories, peering down alleys, following my feet. The long beach at Dee Why drew me down to stroll the tideline, lost in time as I traced the land's edge. From my home now on a bushy ridge I plunge into the evening racket of frogs and kookaburras, my mind both here in the vivid dusk and somewhere else entirely.

In my wanderings I have walked stories into being. Down at the beach, I am in a real place of Norfolk Island pines and spiral shark eggs and footprints filled by the tide, but also a place of memory and invention. My kids still traipse across the hot sand with boogie boards. A character is stopped in her tracks by a glimpse of dangerous blue tentacle.

We move among many stories in Sydney. Writers inscribe the world with the traces of their thoughts, leaving bright trails behind them. Walking out of my own neighbourhood and across the city, I discover the threads laid out across the streets. At the southern pylon of the Harbour Bridge, I imagine encounters between Patyegarang, a local girl, and William Dawes, a First Fleet officer, as they teach each other language. In offering words for things, actions and sensations, they are sharing knowledge about the lives of their people.

Kate Grenville's novel *The Lieutenant* and Ross Gibson's speculative history *26 Views of the Starburst World* placed these images and ideas in my mind. They flicker as I walk the harbour path under the thundering bridge, deepening my sense of what this place holds, its lives and possibilities. In Surry Hills the cottages, terraces and factories call up the world of Ruth Park's *The Harp in the South* and *Poor Man's Orange*, of families and lodgers packed into poor housing, of the many factories drumming, of the men staggering into the lanes from the pubs at six. As my train pulls into Central, I look up into the steep streets and see an old warehouse, and that world shimmers behind this one.

How can this city be understood? This brand-new city, through which the whole world flows, on the edge of an ancient continent. First Nations writers offer a sense of time so deep and present that the city can seem like a thin crust on the living land. The children of diasporas write stories in which the old country and the new, all the generations, breathe in the same bodies. Those once kept to the shadows hoist their stories up in bright flags. Dreamers wander every suburb, finding ways to put their world into words. Imagine a map of these dreams, made like all maps to be read by mind and body.

Readers of the city carry such maps with them. Walking is a means of looking and listening that can be done quietly and at a pace that aids perception, slowly enough to absorb textures and atmospheres, quickly enough to keep the mind alive and the terrain gently shifting. Rebecca Solnit tells us in *Wanderlust: A History of Walking* that the great urban thinker and walker Walter Benjamin was fascinated by cities 'as a kind of organization that could only be perceived by wandering or browsing'. Benjamin was a psychogeographer before the term existed, one interested in the effect of cities on people and in what they make of this influence, culturally and politically. Psychogeography holds walking as its central method of perception: a form of reading – 'browsing' – open to serendipity, to responding to the flows of the city but interested always in going against the grain.

The term 'psychogeography' was coined by Guy Debord of the Situationists, who theorised walking – or the 'dérive' or 'drift' – as a form of resistance to the consumerist organisation of cities. In 'Theory of the Dérive and Definitions' (1958), he wrote:

> In a dérive one or more persons during a certain period drop their relations, their work and leisure activities, and all their other usual motives for movement and action, and let themselves be drawn by the attractions of the terrain and the encounters they find there ... from a dérive point of view, cities have psychogeographical contours, with constant currents, fixed points and vortexes that strongly discourage entry into or exit from certain zones.

Walker-writers have sought to navigate and resist the imperatives and flows of the city, to unearth its real stories by moving through it on foot, in often subversive ways. Merlin Coverley, in *Psychogeography*, discusses those writers of London and Paris who see 'the city as a site of mystery and seek to reveal the true nature that lies beneath the flux of the everyday'. These writers have seen in their wanderings a means to counteract the numbing effects of economic forces, conceiving of urban encounters that drift off prescribed paths. The slowness of walking, necessary for noticing and consideration, is a way to set oneself against the urgings of this frenetic world, in which every moment of our time might be consumed by speed and noise.

In making *Walking Sydney*, I wanted to enlist the key elements of these practices – slow browsing, unearthing, drifting off prescribed paths – to travel more deeply into the life of the city than I had before in my reading and solitary walking. I invited writers whose work engages with many very different locations in Sydney to walk with me, to talk about particular places and how they know them through their writing and lives. Psychogeography has been beholden to the romantic strolling figure of the 'flâneur': solitary, male, aloof. These walkers are friendlier, more engaging companions, willing to share their knowledge and memories, their sense of community, often with urgent purpose. In walking us through their worlds, they make openings in the fabric of the contemporary city through which we might glimpse the experiences, histories and visions that make the dreamlife – the real life – of this city. The walks were true drifts, a few hours' absconding from busy workaday time into the city's full, multidimensional time, each moment of the present imbued with those that led to it and those that might yet come.

The walks begin just south of the city in Aboriginal and working-class heartland, among the old machine shops of the Eveleigh Railway Yards, where artists make their work against the ticking of the development clock. Wiradjuri poet-artist Jazz Money tells the story of the colonial sale of this land to the railways, of the industrial flattening of Gadigal Country, so recently a place of gathering and ceremony. But Country is still present, and we can approach it in a different way: 'When you're going slow and you're observing and you're participating in a tactile way, you are honouring Country.'

A few suburbs across the old industrial fringes of the city are the once-notorious streets of Surry Hills, where busker and thief Iris Webber gained her reputation in the period of sly grog and razor gangs as 'the most violent woman in Sydney'. In her novel *Iris*, Fiona Kelly McGregor tells the story that played out in these terraces and lanes of Iris's attempts to make ends meet; her fierce desire for her lover, Maisie Matthews; and the hidden queer history of 1930s clubs like Black Ada's. As she walks these streets, Fiona's own story interweaves with Iris's: making costumes from fabric bought at the Jewish haberdasheries', throwing Mardi Gras parties in old factories and laneways, living collectively and creatively in the inner city.

Circular Quay and the Rocks, the birthplace of the colony, lie at the other end of Sydney city. In Gail Jones' novel *Five Bells*, she writes of the light and clamour of this place, of characters' personal encounters with the Opera House. This walk, from the curving streets of The Rocks to down amid the timber and steel of Walsh Bay and through the lively crowds at the Quay, captures walks, images and moments in art and literature. Walking amid the flows of people and across time, we encounter the modernist women painters of the Harbour Bridge recording its construction, red-eyed rats emerging from the harbour for the Vivid festival, Joseph Conrad living on board a ship at the western dock and Kenneth Slessor's immersion into the deep time of the harbour.

To the west the harbour becomes a river, narrowing towards the site of Sydney's 'second city', Parramatta, named for the Burramattagal and the eels that swam to this place to breed. Essayist Eda Gunaydin navigates the ever-changing streetscape, where colonial authority seems to linger in the old sandstone buildings, and shiny high-rises and transport projects block off remembered pathways. Eda's mental geography is reconfiguring around the morphing streets, as class and cultural capital take new forms, and the local people live their lives on the frontline of a rapidly changing city.

The recent history of King Street, in the inner-western suburb of Newtown, is of a countercultural past given texture by the colourful Victorian terraces and stores, the treasured graffiti, the signage expressing buildings' former lives. Vanessa Berry is the chronicler of a secret Sydney, interested in what is 'overlooked and odd' in 'the hidden and enigmatic places' of the city, as she writes in *Mirror Sydney: An Atlas of Reflections*. A meander down King Street offers many opportunities to ponder the curiosities of a shop window or the world above the awning, and to appreciate the distinctive form of welcome the suburb offers to generations of young people seeking their tribe.

Out on the edge of Sydney, amid the elements of the coastal suburbs, the mythologies of the beach are shaped. In a cluster of novels by Malcolm Knox, men grapple with notions of success and failure in the beach suburbs of Sydney's north. A recent novel, *Bluebird*, was inspired while Malcolm bobbed on his surfboard at Freshwater, contemplating a derelict house on the headland in a spot where no house should be. A walk around this suburb, much changed since the old days of weekend holiday camps and working-class cottages, takes in the institutions of the beach: the surf club and once-rough pub, the language and instincts of surfing, and the deep and influential memories of danger laid down in childhood encounters with the surf.

Community stories find vivid presence on the streets of Yagoona and Bankstown in the south-west of Sydney. This area has seen vitalising flows of migration, in recent decades largely Vietnamese and Lebanese. Writer and community arts worker Sheila Ngọc Phạm takes us on a walk through suburban streets and into the heart of Vietnamese Bankstown, tracing memory, personal and diasporic, as the daily routines of a life connect with the flows of culture and community. Sheila, in her writing and conversation, responds to the prompts around her – a flag in a garden, a beautiful Ngọc Lũ drum in the centre of a shopping street – opening up portals to intergenerational stories and a wider world.

On the harbour, the bohemian history of Rushcutters Bay and Elizabeth Bay mingles with the city's 'irrepressible geography' of sandstone and water in a walk with Delia Falconer. In *Sydney*, Delia's personal and cultural history, the city's artistic temperament is shaped by its dynamic material life. From the buried marsh of Rushcutters Bay Park, along the barnacle-encrusted sandstone walls of the harbour and up into the streets of colonial manors and Art Deco flats, we discover the city's literary and artistic characters sharing space with rampant figs, colonies of flying foxes and the sandstone forms of Sydney's deep history.

In the 1980s and '90s, Ngarigu woman of the Snowy Mountains and anthropological linguistics scholar Jakelin Troy collected what was known of the local language of the Sydney district at the time of colonisation, and has worked with indigenous languages across the world ever since. This walk moves along a bright bushland ridge from North Willoughby into Middle Cove through Cammeraygal Country; Jaky moves between the cold country near Canberra and this warm coastal place she has known all her life, and brings both lives with her on this walk. She discusses the ways that the Aboriginal groups around Sydney use language as a way of articulating their responsibilities to and relationships with place and with each other: 'Everything you are is embodied in your language.'

In the south-west of Sydney, Max Easton takes us on a walk along the Georges River towards the changing skyline of Liverpool, where we visit the sites of a suburban boyhood, in which a love of rugby league and then a fascination for the subcultural reaches of the fledgling internet laid the foundations of a writing life. Unassuming local nooks – a quiet train station, the towering concrete legs of a disused military bridge, a footy field seemingly suspended in time – give rise to stories of class, subcultural music communities and lives spent trying to make something happen.

From the inner city, Kings Cross emits a homing signal that draws adventurers from far afield. For Melburnian Neal Drinnan an image of the El Alamein Fountain on the nightly news lured him north, where he published novels of gay life amid the suburbs around the Cross. A walk through the sites of this time of uprising and celebration takes us into Darlinghurst, past the old beat of The Wall, through the heart of Oxford Street's Golden Mile – its institutions, celebrations and literary memories – into the magical mire of Surry Hills.

Heading further east, from the lush hidden gully behind Bronte Beach, over the cliffs and through Waverley Cemetery to Clovelly, writer and teacher Beth Yahp explores a writing life forged through the contemplation of small pleasures – walking slowly, feeling one's feet on the ground, and the gifts of a village. In this walk, as in her memoir *Eat First, Talk Later*, larger worlds and histories are accessed through these moments of grounding and connection. The walk leads us towards an old yellow butcher's shop, where writer and social commentator Anne Deveson was Beth's landlady, a 'village elder' around whom a community formed.

Back in Bankstown, Michael Mohammed Ahmad takes us on a tour of the political narratives of recent decades, finishing at his former, much-changed high school, Punchbowl Boys'. This walk provides rich context for his trio of autobiographical novels – *The Tribe*, *The Lebs* and *The Other Half of You* – as well as for his work with Western Sydney writers via the literacy organisation Sweatshop. As we follow a trail from a memorial to an innocent victim of the old gang wars to a beautiful library garden, a story unfolds of the transformative power of language.

Sydney's topography is shaped not just by ocean and harbour but by its network of life-giving rivers. A green and beautiful stretch of the Cooks River, running from Hurlstone Park through Earlwood and Marrickville, provides a place of calm for the residents of the inner west, an opportunity to take long walks alongside mangroves and past secret gardens. Novelist Michelle de Kretser recalls walks with her dog and the sites of inspiration for her stories as we wander the paradise of Greek migrants and the deep time of the rugged cliffs. When Michelle moved here from Melbourne, she found this place unfamiliar in comparison to the more densely recorded locations of eastern Sydney, but soon realised her neighbourhood was 'there to be written about now'.

The final walk takes us from a sculpture gleaming between the trees near the Anzac Memorial in Hyde Park through sites of Aboriginal resistance and community organisation in Redfern and the Block. Euahleyai and Gamillaroi law professor, writer and filmmaker Larissa Behrendt walks us through important sites in the south of the city of activism, art and community.

Moments come to life: the gathering of protestors outside Australian Hall for the Day of Mourning in 1938, a young woman's glimpse through the crowd of Paul Keating making his Redfern Speech, impassioned meetings at the Aboriginal Medical Centre. In the heartland of Redfern and the Block, the 'children of the street marches' learned that 'we are the ones who need to have control of our future'.

All cities change, all the time, but there is an urgency to our reading of the city and its meanings amid the profound pressures of a changing climate and the flux of development that transforms Sydney's familiar shapes overnight. Beaches shrink to rocks in great storms. New towers rise between one visit to the city and the next. As you travel through the city on bridges and freeways, the city reconfigures in fast motion around you. There was a sci-fi film shot in Sydney in the 1990s: *Dark City*. A man in a perpetual night-time city retains no memory of his life from one day to the next. He encounters a group called the Strangers who rearrange the city while the inhabitants are sleeping and re-form their memories and identities. You see glimpses of Sydney sandstone and streetscape as the city morphs but it happens too fast for you to orient yourself.

How to capture memory and meaning before it is severed further from its material foundations? Not in the spirit of preserving a city of the past, but to record what this place has meant and means now, in order to consider, perhaps, what it might yet be.

We all make this city every day – with our lives in it, with the movement of our bodies through its streets and parks and shorelines, and with our thinking, dreaming selves. Rebecca

Solnit writes that for French psychogeographer Jean-Christophe Bailly, the city is 'a collection of stories, a memory of itself made by the walkers of the streets'. I hope that you will enjoy these stories of Sydney made by walking, and take them into those you make, every day, with every step.

YINDYAMARRA

EVELEIGH AND CARRIAGEWORKS

WITH JAZZ MONEY

*

    this city
    thudded
      over site sacred
        curls with ghost
       watch how
      certain places
     bubble with
    horror or
    yearning

*

    I'm looking
      at these maps
      gazing from below
   I'm walking with
  my ghosts
 upon grid
over sewer
  and drain
    sister
        we're marvelling
          at shadows writ
        upon those dreams
      by those
     who walk
    here
    still
    *

– Jazz Money, 'if that ghost is
    still here come morning'

At the heart of the small inner suburb of Eveleigh, tucked between Redfern, Darlington, Newtown and Erskineville, rows of vast weathered-brick machine shops and warehouses line the rail tracks. Operational for a century as the Eveleigh Railway Yards, these remnants of the industrial revolution are in varying stages of renovation and re-use. The clanking and roar of machinery, the men's voices shouting to be heard have been replaced, north of the tracks, by the calm inner-city bustle of weekend markets, art exhibitions and festivals, and cyclists whizzing along the Wilson Street bike path. South of the lines are hip bars and cafes but, as well, quiet, looming workshops with darkened brick and broken windows behind barbed wire. The trains rush through down on the tracks, into the city, out to the suburbs.

This area has been shaped by its Aboriginal and working-class history, its workers drawn to urban employment – shops, quarries, factories – as the city grew. Public-housing residents hold on where they can against the rising tide of gentrification, underway for decades here and in the surrounding suburbs filled with attractive terraces and trees so vigorous their roots rumple the footpaths.

Working away in the fine old Clothing Store building at the western end of the Carriageworks precinct is a group of artists on borrowed time, making art and community in post-industrial spaces as the trains glide past beyond a field of weeds. Among them at the time of this walk is Wiradjuri artist, filmmaker and poet Jazz Money, whose work, earthy and vital, is ever conscious of place and time and what they are telling us, often with urgency. 'these are not spill marks,' Jazz writes, 'but tide rushing in with story to be learnt / across briny mud-rippled flat … if you listen right / you can hear the ancestors walking among us'. Jazz often reads their poetry at public events in Sydney and elsewhere, their stillness and presence making a large audience still and present in return.

Our walk begins in the easternmost pocket of Newtown, on Wilson Street. Away to the south, pretty Burren Street leads down the hill into Erskineville, and yet the station perched on this border is named Macdonaldtown. Marking a vanished suburb, the name is a remnant of 'an incredibly grisly history – the area became synonymous with children being murdered'. In 1892 plumbers discovered human remains in the yard of one of these terraces. Residents John and Sarah Makin were 'baby farmers', entrusted by domestic servants and others with the care of their babies, many of whom they killed. The name of the station is one of the last reminders of the old suburb, a violent history lingering behind its name. It was built for the workers at the Eveleigh Railway Yards and is still in use by students and inner-city residents who flow to and fro under the arches of the rail bridge. The suburb has changed since its industrial days, and more change is coming with the continuing development of the Carriageworks precinct. The inner south of Sydney, long a heartland for Aboriginal and other marginalised communities, becomes a harder place to live as rents and property values skyrocket.

Eveleigh's dramatic reformation began in the early days of the colony and continued apace as steam locomotion arrived. Jazz has researched the origins of the suburb, engaging with Eveleigh's history not as an authority on this place but as a mark of respect by a Wiradjuri person to Gadigal Country and its people. This area, once a place of sand dunes, banksia scrub and wetlands, was replaced by 'Newtown Farm', owned by James Chisholm, whose family was paid a huge sum of money for the land in the 1870s by the NSW government for the building of the railway yards. 'Everyone's very proud of the rail history, but then it reaches the point where you can't go further back in the readily available literature, except for this one thing that I kept reading everywhere, which was that the government paid £100,000 to acquire the site. Who did they pay this money to? It wasn't the Blackfellas. No, it was the descendants of this fellow Chisholm, who'd been awarded the land for his work up on the Hawkesbury, quelling the natives.'

Jazz wrote a poem about this history, '100000', as a site-specific work in the Carriageworks gallery. To make the piece, they spread earth from beneath the buildings on the floor of the gallery and embedded the poem within the soil in white letters, words written on Gadigal Country, made of Country:

> pour upon the soft ground all life under hard new
> liquid stone and preserve for time a history you
> can scratch / £100000 and a time so long stretches
> back / a £ for every year of stolen memory and
> where to bury and where to remember / train
> and carriage all precious relic to preserve and
> enshrine atop just dirt just stone just sand
> unknown /

This was a place of gathering, Jazz's community has explained, 'an ancient place, ceremonial ground. Coming from the west it was the first hill from which you would see the water, and there were ochre pits all around.' When the government bought the land to become the railway yards, the area was a hill. 'They took a steam hammer – this mad piece of industrial machinery – and levelled everything out and then dumped the soil in some quarry that they'd been digging sandstone out of: these crazy interventions in the landscape. The fact that this is a hill just breaks your heart.' In the poem, Jazz writes, 'a place all riches all sand dune water way banksia safe of ceremony of song of care of always / wiped razed and poured'.

Heading down off Wilson Street onto Carriageworks Way, an industrial-scale setting awaits: a broad lot lined with huge brick workshops and storehouses, and you begin to appreciate the enormity of the changes wrought upon the land. Here at the western end it's quiet, and along the road are planted landscaped gardens filled with native grasses. To the north-east, beyond a new apartment block, festivals and exhibitions bring hustle and bustle to the precinct. Art, colonial history and commerce mingle in this de-industrialised space. 'I find the whole area such a fascinating case study of how colonial operations take place. A settler is awarded this incredibly large tract of land, that his kids or grandkids sell back to the government for a tremendous amount of money, which sets a family up for generations. All this land, stolen in living memory. Yet you have these landmark buildings that you can point to and say, "Well, this is the official history."'

There is more history here too – of community, labour and social change. At one time the largest railway workshops in the Southern Hemisphere, employing thousands around the turn of the twentieth century, the Eveleigh Railway Yards were the seeding ground for significant social movement and change. Bringing Aboriginal and other workers from the country to settle in the inner city, the works formed the patterns of settlement and housing in the area. Conditions were brutal, and from the first days Eveleigh was central to the birth of the union movement. Efficiency drives, mass sackings and unpaid shifts led to a walk-off in August 1917, an action that became the roots of the Great Strike, in which almost 100 000 union members across Australia downed tools.

The Railway Yards were in operation until quite recently,

closing in 1988 after a century of operation. 'This was a community where people came together from all different walks of life. Uncle Chicka Madden talks about working down here when he was young, and it being a place where Blackfellas could get work. It's part of the reason Redfern became so important to the community.' Charles Madden, a Gadigal Elder and artist, involved for many years with Redfern Aboriginal community organisations, worked for the railways for fifty years, his story emblematic of the ways in which the history of the city, and the story of the work that has made the city, is also Aboriginal history.

Up at the main precinct, the weathered brick buildings of Carriageworks have been beautifully restored, maintaining a sense of their industrial history in the brick, timber and steel of their construction. Here at the western end, the zone around the Clothing Store building emits an air of intriguing neglect, like so many post-industrial spaces in which artists set up camp while they can. The Store is a large Victorian brick warehouse, a lovely building, long and a couple of generous storeys high, warm in tone, scruffy, fronted by a wooden fence and massive puddles, weeds sprouting all around. This part of the precinct is earmarked for housing, but for now, Jazz and the other artists are free to make art and community in the warehouse's studios. 'If there's a space that no one wants, government gives it to artists because artists will take anything, desperate for a morsel, and then that area becomes desirable. I'd never been in a studio space before; I'd only ever been a solo artist and poet. What happens when you're in a community is so gorgeous. I understand why people really love it.'

It's tricky to access the building, navigating a narrow muddy strip between a wide puddle and the wall. A large, weedy terrace separates it from the tracks where 'the trains come roaring past'. But up a narrow staircase, along a corridor lined with ply, are artists' studios, cavernous spaces full of eccentricity and wonder: intricate weavings of plants, idiosyncratic collections of objects, arcane messages scrawled on walls. In Jazz's studio, light streams in through the tall windows. Along one wall is an immense chalkboard on which their timeline of art projects stretches, with space for conjecture. 'When I'm collaborating with someone, we can just stand here and throw everything at it. It's just so fun to be able to visualise things on a human scale. Also, the luxury of having six by nine metres in Sydney, just to make a mess, will probably never happen again for me.' In every walk in this city, the terrifying cost of space and an accompanying atmosphere of precarity make themselves felt. Even the floods of light from the ceiling-height windows are a brief, extraordinary blessing.

Back out along Carriageworks Way, liminal neglect gives way to the buzz of an event: right now it's Fashion Week, and outlandish outfits and enormous cameras are everywhere. The main building, with its steel remnants, faded brick and cathedral ceilings, houses both commerce and art; gin and shampoo concessions give way to the quiet of the gallery. On the far wall a textile work by one of the Clothing Store artists, Elizabeth Day, fills the huge space. *The Flow of Form: There's a Reason Beyond a Reason. Beyond That There's a Reason* emerged from Day's years of work with women in prisons. Steam locomotives were once housed in these buildings. Across the tracks, at South Eveleigh, the Workers Wall commemorates the men and women undertaking their difficult labour in this place. The energetic jumble of this site, what Jazz calls its 'cheek-to-jowl'-ness, is dizzying.

Up the main stairs to the precinct, you're back on Wilson Street where a courtyard next to the main entrance looks over the buildings and the stretches of open space between them, where rail tracks are still embedded in the road and the crowds mill about. Around the platform is an interpretation space; plaques on the history of the railway yards line the wall. In contrast to this commemoration of industrial processes, Jazz recalls an artwork that hovered above the courtyard during the pandemic: *Remember Me* by Kamilaroi artist Reko Rennie. Its large electric-red letters insisted on Aboriginal memory and continuing survival in this place, 250 years after Cook's landing at Botany Bay. In Jazz's own art and writing, as with their poem written on dirt from beneath the Carriageworks gallery, they too enjoy inviting an audience to consider where they are: 'to consider the layers that are just underneath your feet every day'.

Along Wilson Street, the foot traffic streams towards Redfern Station. Jazz has only recently returned to Sydney, having lived in many places – New York, Hungary, Nepal, Melbourne, the Blue Mountains. They have been 'hodgepodging – it's frenetic to be back. The pace of it, when you're not here, is a puzzle.' One of the ways Jazz connects to place, having lived in thirty houses, is making art. 'When I make something that's intended for a place, I do a heap of research. You can have these deep investments in learning about something. The more you learn about a place, the more satisfying it is to be there. It makes me feel very connected.'

Sydney's special quality, though this sprawling city contains much variety, is a kind of burgeoning or profusion. Jazz has just returned from Melbourne, which smelled different to here: dry. 'I felt, this really smells like Melbourne, which is a place I know and love, and then coming back here, it was warm and lush. Sydney just smells so good for a city. One of the things I really love is that sense that Country is very present, and you feel that if the industrial colonial endeavour was to stop for a moment,

Country would just take all this city back.' Following this thought through, in the poem 'all a homeland' Jazz writes: 'can all this country / taken without ceremony / removed without song / be returned / can this city dissolve / and each stone / with knowing / find its way back to where it belongs'.

Close to the Redfern end of Wilson Street is Shepherd Lane, a cut-through to Abercrombie Street, where frangipanis, ferns, palms and eucalypts overrun narrow garden beds. In late spring, a purple cloud of jacaranda billows amid the bright terraces. On the other side of Wilson Street, as you turn the corner at Little Eveleigh Street towards Redfern Station, a long, grand Victorian building with pristine yellow paint and green ironwork, sits empty and surrounded by fencing. It is the Eveleigh Chief Mechanical Engineer's Office, built in 1887, soon after Chisholm's sale of the land. It has been empty for years, and it's easy to fall into conjecturing what you could do with such a space, envisioning the long shady balconies filled with people laughing on a weekend afternoon.

Around the corner, Little Eveleigh Street is pristine and paved, offering new pedestrian access to Redfern Station. *The Big Issue* office has gone, the well-loved terraces spruced up. A strange gallery window at the front of a garage survives, happily. A couple of the newly painted terraces look straight into the new entrance to Redfern Station, where commuters and students spill through the electronic gates. Plaques commemorating Aboriginal community history are embedded in the tiles beneath our feet.

There is a pleasure in joining the stream of students walking west along Lawson Street towards the university. Walking is a marker and expression of freedom, and to walk collectively can be energising. Jazz, in their travels in different countries, found joy in those places where the street was welcoming to walkers.

'Whenever you felt like you could just walk down the street, it was a better place to be', places developed 'with the street in mind and with people in mind, with community at the centre'. An extra gift: singing in the streets, songs familiar to the entire community. While in Ireland, the place of Jazz's maternal heritage, they were inspired 'to be in proximity to the joy that comes through people making music for the pleasure of making music, not for economic outcome', to share in this pleasure of 'a place where everyone knows the words'. Jazz has recreated the joy of many voices singing in a work for World Pride, in which a mass choir of more than 400 people sang the words to their piece 'This is How We Love'. 'Even now when I listen to the recordings or watch that footage, it's just beyond anything: the power of people and the power of voices and that shared breath, the communion that comes with singing.'

On the final stretch of the circuit, along Codrington Street in Darlington, the University of Sydney swallows the streetscape: the gym, the glossy Business School. In recent decades, the large city universities have reshaped the streets and demographics of these suburbs as dramatically as industry did in the past. We move through the city amid the flow of time, its presence unearthed as we walk: the old land and ways, the workers, the spaces of meeting and making, the changes underway and those to come.

What does it mean for Jazz to walk through a place, as an artist, as a person, to consider its meanings and stories? 'My primary mode of transport is my feet. It's the way that I orient in the world. It's also the way to honour being in place. When you're going slow and you're observing and you're participating in a tactile way, you are honouring Country. We have this philosophy in Wiradjuri – Yindyamarra. It's not very easy to translate, but at its simplest it means to go slowly and respectfully. It's a whole philosophical worldview that involves listening and being deeply invested in the things that you do, and being invested in improving the world around you as you do these things. It's where so much of my work comes from – as a writer and as a person who makes art – just thinking deeply about place. People are made up by the narratives that we tell and that happens on a political, social, personal, interpersonal level. I think you understand those knowledges when you go slowly. If you're interested in story and the way that stories operate, there isn't a square centimetre of this continent that isn't rich with it, and with story that goes back to the first sunrise.'

HISTORY BENEATH YOUR FEET

SURRY HILLS

WITH FIONA KELLY McGREGOR

Clisdell Street, Maisie had said. Parallel to Elizabeth just before Redfern, a narrow street that swooped like the Big Dipper from Belvoir Street down to Devonshire. Maisie's friend lived in a Georgian terrace right at the bottom of the street, the red brick blackened with factory soot. It had been so hot and dry the smog felt solid, the sun burning through like a cigarette tip, machinery all around going clunkclunk-clunkclunk, clunkclunk-clunkclunk.

– Fiona Kelly McGregor, *Iris*

Surry Hills flickers into view as the train emerges from under the Goulburn Street carpark: canyons of streets, glimpses of old warehouses among the office blocks, shafts of light pouring down the walls to the footpaths. In the evening, the shadows of trees pattern sandstone walls and the ends of flaky terraces; golden light flashes on windows as the traffic lights and bar signs strike up their glow against the dark.

The clay ridges and slopes of Surry Hills, close to the city but away from the water, have been shaped since colonisation by industrial and slum history. There are stories here older than writing, and those that have flooded in since the nineteenth century with the factory and quarry workers, Chinese grocers and herbalists, notorious crims, working girls and coppers.

In the last century the poets of these streets were Kylie Tennant and Ruth Park, their work crowded with the tough, poor occupants of rotting terraces, smoky factories and the pubs around Central Station. In recent decades it is Fiona Kelly McGregor's writing that has told the stories of the warehouses and terraces, the steep streets and dark alleys: in her work, artists, queer people, wives fleeing the suburbs and interwar gangsters all seek the freedom and licence of the inner city.

Fiona's essay 'Surro' spreads the layers of experience, real and imaginary, across the streetscape. On the cusp of the new millennium, artists, musicians, DJs and sex workers made creative use of the window in time when the old warehouses and factories were cheap or free to occupy, and energy was available to make art, pleasure and radical moments. Here and in *Buried Not Dead*, the essay collection in which it appears, Fiona conjures the scenes of the late twentieth century: of creativity cooked up in the pubs and warehouses of Surry Hills, of art and activism springing from the streets.

The ghosts of earlier decades walk among these scenes: the characters of criminal Sydney from the desperate '30s, in particular the headstrong queer busker and thief, Iris Webber, who came to be known as 'the most violent woman in Sydney'. This resourceful and gutsy woman from Glen Innes became the protagonist of a novel: *Iris*. 'She drew me in through sheer force of personality,' Fiona writes of her discovery. 'To then find so much of her history directly beneath my feet increased the sense of ghostly calling.' Vivid avatars of Iris's milieu walk these hills too: Kate Leigh, Tilly Devine's great rival, amassing a fortune from sly grog in the early decades of the six o'clock swill; Maisie Matthews, working girl and lover of Iris and violent crims Bill Smillie and Slim Maley, both of whom Iris shot.

Nearly a century ago, when notorious slums swallowed pockets of Surry Hills, there was a good side of Devonshire Street and a bad, and the bad side is where many of the key scenes of Iris's criminal history played out. A walk towards the slum streets of Iris's days begins at the new light rail stop on Chalmers Street outside Central Station, where the flow of people is endless and the modernist wedge of the Sydney Dental Hospital gleams pale at the intersection. Fiona has Iris arrive at Central with no money or work, in the midst of Depression-era scenes: 'All along the gangplank men held signs asking for work. A woman sat on a butterbox with a bawling baby on her lap and a toddler next to her, muttering *Spare change?*' Today, in this city awash with money, commuters flood under the sandstone bridge towards the buses and the city, past people without homes sleeping rough under cardboard.

Iris survives, the records show, through busking and thieving. In Fiona's novel, Iris also engages in sex work, living first in a brothel and ending up in the slums between Elizabeth Street and Cleveland Street, soon to fall for Maisie Matthews, her neighbour's friend and gangster's moll. Maisie came out of the notorious Parramatta Girls Home to a life on the streets, and the court records connect her to a terrace on Buckingham Street, a few minutes' walk south of Central. In *Iris*, this is where Maisie takes in customers. The house is still there, in a street of pretty terraces with a smart hole-in-the-wall cafe. Along the back runs an alleyway: 'Here, I've got Iris watching for Maisie.' Fiona indicates an upstairs window. 'I imagined Maisie working in that back room. Clients would come in and out here.' The comings and goings in the night, Iris's longings, spring up amid the steel roller doors and neat rows of household bins.

Five minutes' walk away, on the other side of Elizabeth Street, was Iris's place at 6 Clisdell Street, flattened now with the razing of the slums. To reach the spot you walk along Butt Street, an alleyway of slick warehouse apartments and a real estate office, where Maisie's gangster boyfriend Bill Smillie was eventually killed by shooting, probably by professional thieves George Dempsey and John McIvor. In 'Surro': 'You are walking towards Clisdell Street in August 1940, and on the left in the gutter is the corpse of Bill Smillie, gambler, gunman, SP standover. Next to his body is a dead cat.' We're deep in Iris territory, a mix of the real and imagined. The ghosts of Bill and accompanying cat lie at the back of Sadie Pinn's grocery, where fictional Iris offloaded stolen goods. Around the front on Devonshire Street, Sadie's place is a flaky old shopfront between terraces and mansions, grilled windows blank to the tram passengers, its history quiet. And just beyond, on the other side of the street, is the house in which Bill lived from birth until his violent death, with many of the years between a reign of violence on behalf of his boss in the 1920s, Kate Leigh.

Here in the lane, as we note the site of a gangster's grim passing, a performance artist and friend from the old days wanders through and stops to catch up with Fiona. It's a reminder that we walk through many pasts, the streets continually changing, peopled with artists and gangsters, lovers and thieves.

At the end of Butt Street is Iris's street, Clisdell. 'This was a notorious slum – the steepness of the hill would have made the houses down the bottom here even worse than elsewhere, because everything would have run down these hills. They didn't have sewerage – that started out up on the ridge in the big houses on Crown Street. A lot of these little hovels would have had rubbish running in the drains.' A wall splits Clisdell along its length, one side of the street higher. Where Iris's house stood, on the high side, is Sydney's largest public-housing estate, Northcott, campaigned for by Ruth Park and opened by the Queen in 1963.

Since then the estate has replaced the squalid conditions of the early twentieth-century cottages and lanes with its own communities and sometimes notoriety. There was a multiple shooting in 1990 – 'the Surry Hills massacre' – and in 2001 the grisly discovery of a double murder. Fiona's friends, the 'queer kids', had a house down here in Brumby Street, and they told her 'how full-on this area was in the '90s'. At the turn of the century, Fiona spent a lot of time in the warehouse of her girlfriend nearby, and helicopters, spotlights on the flats, woke them often. 'It was police harassment, pure and simple. It always accelerated before a state election.' But the flats themselves were great, the result of good intentions and design; in 'Surro': 'The old red brick flats are light, airy and well insulated. Theatre critic Jim Waites lived in one, happy in that mix of crims and eccentrics, urban Aboriginals, long-term HIV positive poofs, druggies and the generally poor.'

Walking from the dip of Clisdell Street between the estate and the streets of terraces up towards the bright red wall of the Belvoir St Theatre takes us back into Iris's time. Before Bill Smillie was killed in the alley, Iris had a go. 'When Iris shot Bill, I had her chasing him up here.' In the novel, Bill turns up at the house of Iris's next-door neighbour on Clisdell Street looking for Iris and Maisie, and Iris runs next door to fetch her Browning:

> He ran up to Belvoir Street, I was losing ground, the breath like fire in my lungs. I shot at him and he ran faster, I rounded the corner and Bill was right there closer than I expected, grabbing the end of the rifle. *I'm gonna kill you you fucken bastard!* I screamed and pulled the trigger.

This steep street 'would have been in a shitty state'; it would take will and fury to run up it, chasing a violent man wielding a blade, defending your woman and your right to love her.

'She's righteous. She's not having it. Even though the world is saying at every turn, "You need to accept this." She was like that till the end of her days.'

The terrace- and warehouse-lined streets and lanes between Clisdell and Elizabeth Streets are as romantic as anywhere in the inner city, crowded with trees, the colours of the terraces soft in the sun, iron lacework glinting on the balconies. In the '30s of *Iris*, working girls took clients into the dark, squalid alleys – or 'poo lanes' – where they might make their living, or be robbed or bashed, out of sight. The nearby pubs – the Invicta, the Southern Cross Hotel – emptied out in the evenings, 'men coming off the trains at Central, coming out of the factories', and the work began.

Painted posters on the theatre wall at the top of the hill advertise plays, recent and soon to arrive. Walking east you skirt a small park providing green space for the residents of the public-housing units all around, but right here, where Belvoir Street meets Lansdowne, was sly-grog boss Kate Leigh's grand terrace at 2 Lansdowne Street. Leigh, known as the queen of Surry Hills, ran more than twenty sly groggeries in the area, her business protected by the likes of Iris's rival Smillie and throughout the '20s by the notorious razor gangs. A famous photograph shows the house, Kate on the balcony with Father Christmas, showering Christmas gifts on local residents. 'She was at the top of the hill, strategically a good place to be – and it was a very big house – an old butcher or baker. It went back a long way. It had a garage, and a coolroom that the butcher had used. That's where in the novel they're bottling sly grog, and diluting it.'

Fiona worked with old maps to recreate this area – the old Strawberry Hills – comparing old and new to create a palimpsest. 'The Pottery Hotel was here, and a sports arena.

This whole area of the housing commission was a warren of streets: Little Pearl, O'Sullivan, Dawson went further up. There was nothing to be done with this place; they razed it.'

Heading through the park, where residents of the flats share a bench and a laugh, and a girl with a curtain of hair for privacy reads a textbook, we're briefly back in the futuristic-feeling present, on smartened-up Devonshire Street – a sleek tram rushing quietly along the new paving – before dipping back into the recent past. Just after the junction with Crown Street, the Brackenbury & Austin, a small red warehouse occupied by architects' offices, was the home of Fiona's girlfriend and other tenants, when all around was semi-commercial. 'They used to close off Wilshire Street each year during the Mardi Gras festival for a Sunday arvo party, creating a dance floor and DJ booth, stringing up a mirror ball and putting on shows. They'd leaflet all of the surrounding houses and invite them. Nobody objected. Afterwards we cleaned the street so that it was cleaner than before, and then gradually, at the beginning of the twenty-first century, the police started to drive past. After a few years, they said, "You're going to get fined 40,000 dollars for going over the noise restrictions."'

At around this time Fiona made a discovery that brought the history of these streets to life. In 2001, she visited an exhibition of queer history at NSW Parliament House, staged by archivist and founder of activist group the Sisters of Perpetual Indulgence, Fabian LoSchiavo. 'I was always interested in the interwar period in terms of politics and art. It was one of those flashpoints for queer people when it seemed like we had a kind of cultural community in some parts of the world, despite generally being criminalised. It's hard to find working-class women who lived openly as queer – they were overwhelmingly from bohemian or upper-class circles, congregating in Europe.

But to discover someone from this grungy old working-class criminal world who was open about her relationships with women – I'd never found anything like that anywhere.'

In her doctoral thesis, Fiona writes:

> Iris haunted me. How exciting to have had a queer girl gangster in my native city, who had fought over her "moll" ... The title of the exhibition, "Mad, Bad and Dangerous to Know", indicated how queers in history have been considered, as well as resurrected ... Just as we have reclaimed pejoratives ... so too we reclaim our outlaws.

But the relationships writers have with their subjects, particularly real historical figures, is never straightforward. Unlike Tilly and Kate, who built their empires on ruthless ambition, Iris was not actually a gangster, as Fiona's research soon revealed. She was 'a petty crim with few prospects, living day by day, hand to mouth. I quickly realised I'd romanticised her.'

Up on Crown Street the bustle of people coming and going from restaurants and gelato shops masks the secret lives played out in these houses and streets over the decades. A block from Devonshire there's a yellow corner house, a cafe occupying its street level. Iris's lover Maisie took a room here after time in jail for a slashing crime. The side door is open: narrow stairs wind around to upstairs rooms and down to a cellar. Fiona has ventured further inside: 'When you get to the top, the ceiling drops and you're crouching – the stairs are even narrower. I made her room the tiniest, pokiest room at the back.' Maisie's lover after Bill, Slim Maley, also moved in after doing time for slashing. Here he hit her with an enamel basin, and Maisie was rescued by Iris and her neighbour Kathleen McLennan, leading to further violence.

Sexism took both extreme and casual forms, then as now. Fiona gained some of the textures of this dynamic from lifelong Surry Hills resident Joyce Regowski, born in the late 1920s and a girl when Iris and co roamed the streets, living in the same house then as now, a large terrace in Riley Street. In Iris's childhood in the novel, it was steaks for the boys and sausages for the girls, a detail gleaned from talking to Joyce. Her family made the move up the hill from down on the slum side of Devonshire Street when her father won big on the races. 'As a working-class girl, Joyce went off to work in a shop when she was fourteen. She walked a very particular route to the shop, which was on this side of Devonshire Street, and because she was a girl, and Catholic, her movements were tightly controlled. The boys had a lot of freedom and the girls didn't.' This difference meant she was protected from knowledge of what really went on around her, even though she passed by people every day making their living from booze, cocaine and sex work, and protecting their territory with razors and guns.

Joyce's terrace is still here, large and white, stretching out at the back into the lane. There's a school nearby; you can hear kids playing beyond the lovely trees. In *Iris* the grand old terraces along Crown and Riley Streets house sly groggeries, and the girls are doing what they can to survive. Nowadays the drinking is more organised, centred on the Clock and the Dolphin pubs. The gleaming glass library stuffed with huge tropical plants faces the park between the watering holes. Mature trees shade walkers and cyclists. First Nations Sydney Swans footballer Adam Goodes looks over the busy streets from a mural at the corner of Foveaux Street.

Heading through the laneways amid terraces and warehouses, Fiona's memories of friends and parties rise up from the footpaths. Down on the bend of Bourke Street, the

Carrington, a pub with people sitting outside watching the street over a beer, was where in the '90s 'we plotted our first dance parties. In those days, it was grungy. A bunch of old geezers were the only people drinking at the bar, and we could go in and set up decks and have a little Sunday-afternoon thing.' Down around Foveaux and Albion Streets, the rag trade still operated in the warehouses, 'often run by generations of Jewish families, with the most obscure haberdashery items – we'd get them for costumes for parties'. On a pretty side street behind Foveaux, where a three-storey terrace is skirted with a profusion of plants, friends transformed their house for a party one night. 'When you opened the door it was all white – you couldn't see the room's dimensions, it was totally disorienting. The only way in was to get on your knees and crawl through a tunnel. It was really claustrophobic – then when you popped out the other end, you saw you were in a room full of white balloons up to shoulder height. All you could see were these balloons and people's heads, everybody looking shocked and delighted. It was surreal.'

Iris is present amid the more recent memories. On Belmore Street is a beautiful Federation warehouse bearing the words 'Truscott and Sons Pty Ltd. High Grade Printing Ink Manufacturers'. 'Iris can smell the ink in the street: this is the printing and newspaper district.' *The Australian* newspaper's office is nearby, down near Foveaux. Another warehouse looks abandoned, emitting 'the smell of bad rentals, mouldy old carpet, cockroaches. Someone told me that squats had started up again.' On the corner of Commonwealth and Campbell Streets is Berman House, emblazoned with the legend 'Imperial Slacks'. Here an artist collective thrived in the '90s. A story in the *Sydney Morning Herald* by a visiting performer described those times:

Members of the collective worked, exhibited art, hosted performance nights and lived in the centre of a city that was eliminating such spaces in favour of upmarket 'New York loft-style' apartments with sky-high rents. For two years, though, Imperial Slacks was the most dazzling, exotic and dangerous art headquarters in town.

At the end of the loop back down to Central on Wentworth Street was another important site of artistic transformation – and, for fictional Iris, of personal transformation too: Black Ada's. Ada went by various names, including Samuel Roy Pearce and Ray Sayles, 'and had been a vaudeville star: radio, stage, dancing and singing. Descendants of this person are prolific, and include gay Aboriginal Sydneysider Simon Jordan', with whom McGregor connected on social media after publishing *Iris*. Roy/Ray/Ada 'ran a dancing academy, legitimately. And then after hours, it became Black Ada's.' Here gay men could dance and be together, ever alert to the urgency of swiftly concealing the scene in case of a police raid. Fiona discovered in her research 'an attendee recalling a sprinkling of "know-all-girls" in the crowd', and interpolated queer female characters into her fictional version of the nightclub. On the dance floor, Iris kisses Maisie, and

> it seemed the most natural thing then someone yelled, VICE! and a shiver went through the crowd ... I saw the pianist remove his pearls and lipstick with one hand switching to a waltz with the other ... Ada appeared from out the back in trousers minus wig and lipstick and began to shout dance instructions from the stage to the dwindling crowd.

As if to underscore the way in which the law and something sweeter and wilder occupy the same nooks in the city, just around the corner sprawls the Sydney Police Centre, a brutalist complex of authority and control laid across the site of the first Surry Hills land resumption and 'built right on top of old opium dens, brothels – the slums'.

These streets, close to the growl of the city and the trains trundling in and out of Central, are never quiet. Here comes Iris with her accordion to make a little money on the streets around the station, just as buskers do today. Ada's voice calls out instructions amid the rumble of Wentworth Street. Performers are visible in silhouette in the broken windows of old warehouses. 'I moved to Redfern thirteen years ago and since I've been there, working on *Iris*, I would often walk over to Surry Hills, or I'd be walking home from being out, through the dark streets, and I'd go down and walk past Clisdell Street. The streets are boiling with layers of life. Readers say they feel that way now when they walk these streets. That's what I wanted to do, to make people aware of what was happening here before. That's the power of characters. They enter your life like people that you've met.'

VERTICALS OF LIGHT

THE ROCKS, WALSH BAY
AND CIRCULAR QUAY

WITH
GAIL JONES

> There was confusion at first, the shock of sudden light, all the signs, all the clamour. But the vista resolved and she saw before her the row of ferry ports, each looking like a primary-colour holiday pavilion, and the boats, bobbing, their green and yellow forms toy-like, arriving, absorbing slow lines of passengers, departing. With a trampoline heart she saw the Bridge to her left: its modern shape, its optimistic uparching.
>
> – Gail Jones, *Five Bells*

People and time course and flood at Warrane, or Sydney Cove. On these shores, for thousands of years, people moved on foot to the fresh stream and the harbour, paddled out into the deeper water and to the far shore in nawi. Then the British landed at the cove, bringing with them a break in the flow of time and, over the centuries, millions of people, continually passing through this place. On a map of modern Sydney, the ferry routes spread out from their tight cluster at Circular Quay like electrical wires. At the Overseas Passenger Terminal on the western dock, hulking cruise ships dwarf the ferries and pleasure boats, spilling and drawing in crowds of international visitors. Towers of glass and steel push little cranes ever higher into the sky as time wells beneath the layers of the city.

The jumble and spectacle of the Quay form the setting of Gail Jones' novel *Five Bells*. Ellie, a new arrival from Western Australia, is filled with 'corny delight' amid the sounds of the ferries and trains, a child's squeal, a didgeridoo, a 'melody of voices' on the water, feeling herself to be 'at the intersection of so many currents of information … breathing in light'. The novel is named for the elegiac Kenneth Slessor poem, in which time floods but does not flow as memories of a friend, drowned Joe Lynch, rise from the dark waters of the harbour between a ship's bells. In Gail's novel, too, time is watery, the past welling in four strangers moving through the Quay on a sweltering Sydney day, their paths overlapping with that of a lost child.

Walking with Gail, these flows and connections through time, between shores and countries, are everywhere present. Beginning on George Street in The Rocks, amid the crooked streets of nineteenth-century warehouses and terraces, the modern city is visible in glimpses: a shiny tower at the end of a hilly street, the steel arch of the Harbour Bridge curving above the roofs. Gail calls to mind modernist women painters of the Bridge – Dorrit Black and Grace Cossington Smith – who liked to paint it from across the water at Milsons Point, as a century ago 'the arms came together in embrace'. She is particularly attached to Dorrit Black's 1930 painting *The Bridge*, that has 'the arms not quite touching'. The first Australian Cubist landscape, it brings the influences of Black's European training to the local scene. It seems of its time but also outside specific time, blending the light of different times of day, and of different centuries too, in a clipper, a telegraph pole. The arms reach, drawing the shores of the harbour together.

The new Sydney is continually laid over the old, the Bridge rising from the rubble of old streets and homes. Above the iron roofs of a row of terraces and the Mercantile Hotel hover the brutalist concrete blocks of the Sirius apartment building, built in the late '70s to house residents of The Rocks displaced by development. Even before these disruptions, Gail says, this area was long 'disparaged as a working-class site. In 1900, The Rocks area was the site of a bubonic plague outbreak in Sydney. Over 35 000 rats were caught here and there exist photographs in the Mitchell Library of rat catchers standing proudly with their piles of dead trophies. This area was whitewashed and quarantined as a place of contamination.' It is a neighbourhood inhabited by the wealthy now: the Sirius has been refurbished, its community moved on and, like the large Victorian terraces that line these hilly streets, its apartments sold for extraordinary prices.

At the intersection of George Street with Hickson Road, Sydney's maritime history is all around in the grand old stores lining the harbour and the Mariners' Church bearing the legend 'The Rawson Institute for Seamen'. In the late 1870s, a famous literary sailor, Joseph Conrad, made his home for five months on the *Duke of Sutherland* here on the western dock of the Quay. Gail's novel *One Another* imaginatively revisits his life, including those months living here on the water. 'He wrote most of his first novel in Circular Quay, on board. He was fascinated by The Rocks. There were Chinese vendors here – he enjoyed the Chinese food – and also listening to people walking up George Street, calling out, "Saveloys!" Probably in a Cockney accent: *saveloys*!' Conrad was bewitched by the city and harbour, returning several times. He wrote of Sydney Harbour in *The Mirror of the Sea* that it was 'one of the finest, most beautiful, vast, and safe bays the sun ever shone upon'.

The roar of the Bridge grows louder as you follow George Street north to stand under its impressive span. There's a wonderful sound here, a rhythmic rumble, as vehicles roar above, and a sudden absence of people, though the pylons of the Bridge and its high roadway photogenically frame the views of harbour and Opera House to the east and a row of smart terraces to the west. 'Six million rivets!' Gail says, standing under the thundering Bridge. 'I find it so exciting. The first time I crossed the Bridge, I felt so modern.' Before moving to Sydney from Perth, Gail was intrigued by it, researching its construction for a talk about creativity. The green-and-gold ferries too are enchanting in their toylike appearance: 'These relics in the centre of the modern city – so charming. One of the things I love is how early the ferries and railways were established. There's a formal and aesthetic vision here of fanning out from the Quay. It was always a place of vibrant movement between countries and shores.'

One of Gail's literary associations for the Quay is Walt Whitman's poem 'Crossing Brooklyn Ferry'. In the poem, Whitman evokes a city – mid-nineteenth-century New York – bustling with industry and seagoing activity. Many of its details might describe the phase of Sydney familiar to Conrad. Crossing the East River where the Brooklyn Bridge would be built a few decades later, he takes in 'the white sails of schooners and sloops', 'the sailors at work in the rigging', 'large and small steamers in motion', 'the white wake left by the passage, the quick tremulous whirl of the wheels', 'the flags of all nations', 'the granite storehouses by the docks'. The fuel of his vision is a connection with the travelling crowds now and across time:

> Crowds of men and women attired in the
> usual costumes, how curious you are to me!
> On the ferry-boats the hundreds and
> hundreds that cross, returning home, are
> more curious to me than you suppose,
> And you that shall cross from shore to shore
> years hence are more to me, and more in my
> meditations, than you might suppose.

'Supposition is here a kind of imaginative largesse,' Gail says, 'summoned with affection, solidarity and timeless fellow-feeling. There's a photograph by Max Dupain of people disembarking from the ferry in a strong shaft of light. You see them walking from the ferry into the city. I find this very moving, the image of people flowing in and out of lit and shadowed spaces.' In *Five Bells* Ellie too is captured by the emotional resonance of people on the move, heading out to 'wander the city, finding the pleasure of eddying crowds and the wayward motions of human traffic, their tidal sweeps at traffic lights, their rhythmic currents of locomotion'. There are photographs at Wynyard Station as you travel down the escalator, of commuters in the fashions of the '30s or '40s, themselves moving down the escalator: other workers, people of Sydney, beginning their day, across time.

Out on Lower Fort Street, the surreal painted face at Luna Park gates leers from across the water. If you turn to the south, the dark shining tower at Barangaroo rises into the sky at the end of a street of terraces, chimneys and trees, disrupting the Victorian scale. The pristine row of terraces opposite the pylons of the Bridge, once public housing, now sold on, 'are well preserved and often appear in movies. In Peter Weir's film *The Last Wave*, an old Aboriginal man is hidden in one of these terraces, chanting mysteriously. He is speaking in his own language, apparently summoning spirits of place, but Weir implies he is doomed to be marginalised and misunderstood.'

One of Sydney's hair-raisingly steep sets of stone stairs plunges down off Lower Fort Street past the end terrace. Above and behind is the swoop of the Bridge. Below are the grey-blue finger wharves at Walsh Bay, stretching towards Harry Seidler's modernist Blues Point Tower on the opposite shore. The old wharves, boarded up in the 1970s, later revivified, house several arts organisations, including Bangarra Dance Theatre and Bell Shakespeare; across the road is the Sydney

Theatre Company. As shows begin and end down here in the evenings, Hickson Road is alive with people milling about among the wharves and old warehouses. At the bottom of the stairs, in the harbour, during the Vivid light festival, was *Rats*: 'an installation of rats with bright-red eyes. You peered into the darkness and saw them coming ashore: a gothic and disturbing element, in the context of Vivid. The cultural theorist Margaret Cohen considers how we know cities. She says that Paris is so well known because the Blue Guides have told us where to go – everyone's seen the Eiffel Tower. But imagine a Black Guide, she says, which describes the uncanny, the irrational, and the repressed elements of the city. She's interested in "profane illumination" – Walter Benjamin's phrase to describe things flashing up to us in a "moment of danger", the moment of seeing into the heart of things.'

Rats was another memento of the bubonic plague outbreak that shaped the built form of the area in the demolition of buildings and the construction of a new seawall. In the daytime, the wall is beautiful, a part-organic structure, its sandstone encrusted with oysters and barnacles. The wooden piers too on which the wharves and jetties sit create a kind of harbour magic. There's a dull sound as boats thud against them that is a part of the harbour's atmosphere. And on the jetties, their backs to the arty goings-on inside these wharves, are often groups of boys or men fishing. 'One of the things about a watery city is that it has so many purposes: some are for pleasure and some are more material.' Scenes of childhood surface amid the jetties and water; Gail lived for a time when young in the Kimberley: 'We did a lot of fishing when I was a child. It was one of our main sources of food.'

Wandering through the arches of the wharves you can peek into rehearsal rooms, drift by the cafe and wonder who among the patrons is a dancer, an actor, a cellist. The mix of wood and steel in the old piers, the old and new, is thrilling. The last of the wharves, Piers 8 and 9, are striking, with three peaked roofs and industrial gantries jutting out above the boardwalk. 'There's something about industrial architecture that's very compelling. Look at the symmetry and the shapes. That's a beautiful building.' Down here at Walsh Bay, the people ebb and flow. It can be very busy, amid festivals and events, but often surprisingly quiet. Walking the slanted and weathered boards, friendly beneath the feet, the precinct is 'remarkably empty of people – we're at the very centre of a major city. Sometimes you can find places of repose. I used to come here and read. You can just sit on a jetty, with your legs dangling, and be left alone, seeing the ferries in the distance.'

Beyond the wharves, a handsome nineteenth-century warehouse building – now the Port Authority of New South Wales – marks the border between Walsh Bay and the new Barangaroo development and park. This area along the northeastern shore of Darling Harbour has been redeveloped in recent years from the wharves of the Hungry Mile, where in the Depression workers wandered from dock to dock looking for work, and in the late twentieth century you could look down from the high office blocks of the city to see the tiny cars spewing out of the cargo ships and taking their place in the immense pattern of the parking lots. There is a pleasant park – Barangaroo Reserve – covering the point and a long walkway taking you all the way to Chinatown at the southern end of the city. The Crown Sydney tower looms as you move south, and the skyscrapers clustered around it, a grim sort of monumentalism, 'out of sympathy with what surrounds it'.

We turn back towards the Quay along Hickson Road past the Sydney Theatre Company and Gail recalls the famous writerly walk of Virginia Woolf's essay 'Street Haunting'. 'The whole purpose of her walk is to buy a pencil. She wanders in errant, strange ways through the streets of London. It's symbolic that she wants to buy the instrument that will then register her own walk – because it's clearly a pretext. I make up those too. I tend to vary my habitual routes and am rarely direct.' In Woolf's essay, when one heads out for a walk, 'We are no longer quite ourselves. As we step out of the house on a fine evening between four and six, we shed the self our friends know us by ...' On the streets of London, Woolf glimpses and mingles with other lives; 'the shell-like covering' that makes a person distinct is abandoned so that the walker become a 'central oyster of perceptiveness, an enormous eye'. It is thrilling to be on this walk with this wonderful writer of fiction, as she gleans lives and dispositions and histories from the sight of a person on a balcony, a couple mid-argument in a shop. A modernist consciousness sets itself loose on the streets, perceiving and processing the contingencies of the day into something new. 'Into each of these lives one could penetrate a little way,' Woolf writes, 'far enough to give oneself the illusion that one is not tethered to a single mind, but can put on briefly for a few minutes the bodies and minds of others.'

Following Hickson Road around Dawes Point, the thunder of the Bridge swallows you once more. This point was recorded as Tarra in Gadigal language, in the notebooks of First Fleet polymath William Dawes, and later known as Dawes Point for the camp and observatory he made in this location. This is where he recorded conversations with the Aboriginal girl Patyegarang, the source of much of what is known of the language of the Sydney area. Here are a bright park and walkway, and a bride, her veil streaming in the breeze off the water, picking up the pale shimmer of the Opera House across the Quay. Along the path, busy with runners and office workers, are the layers of the city: the ten peaks of the early colonial warehouse Campbell's Stores in the foreground, towers and cranes on concrete platforms shooting up beyond.

Observations about the day, decisions about paths to take, bring associations between walking and writing. Writing, like walking, makes use of the materials to hand. 'We improvise all the time with what randomly comes our way. That seems to me a necessary skill for what we do, a craft skill.' As with a walk, writing can be prone to the diversion. 'Swerving, veering, being intercepted, being overtaken. There's a contradiction in psychogeography between what is sometimes called "occulted movement", movement that is mysterious, where you're setting in motion the deep inner self; and another version that is all about intention. A personal psychogeography is a different model of noticing, where you are activating a kind of dissident self. I love the idea that there is intention and volition and even political purpose to it: to notice what you value, why you value it, and what kinds of discarded value we might want to recover. We make a city our own by noticing.'

The way is closed for a cordoned queue of passengers dragging rumbling cases into the Overseas Passenger Terminal, about to be consumed by the cruise ship, nine storeys high, which has carved out chunks of the view from every angle. This ship is too large to see the people on board. Contrast this with photographs like David Moore's *Migrants Arriving in Sydney*, which seems to capture the moment of uncertainty on the faces of people looking out over the railing. 'Those photos are so touching, so poignant.' Gail recalls her own passage to a new life by boat. 'When we first moved to the Kimberley, we went by state ship. There was no sealed road to Broome. It took a week to go from Perth to the Kimberley on a cargo ship –

nothing like as big as this one. The passage always seemed like such an adventure, especially when we went through a cyclone, with huge waves coming over the deck.'

The Quay is a place of encounter for many, for arrival from overseas, or as the entry point to the city from the train and wharves. 'When I arrived here Circular Quay was often described as tawdry, a depleted space for tourists – too busy and full of souvenir shops, and ugly. I wanted to contest this – spaces are multiple, various and contradictory.' In *Five Bells*, we are introduced to characters, their dispositions and the ways in which they carry their histories through their responses to the Opera House. Gail says, 'Aesthetic pleasure lies at the centre of the fictional space. I have witnessed visitors jolt back in a kind of surprise when they first see the Opera House.' She wanted to honour that 'pressure of rapture – the sudden, unexpected rapture of being in a crowd where people are gawking at monuments and taking photographs of something that they've only ever seen on a postcard. This is a model of encounter to be cherished.' Being among the crowd as it responds to the 'aesthetic monument' can be very moving. The Opera House is often transformed by images designed to play over its surfaces; so too, during Vivid, is the Museum of Contemporary Art, on the other side of Circular Quay. 'Watching that changing façade,' Gail has been 'made tearful by the spectacle. Part of it is being within the crowd; feeling the pleasure of collective excitement.'

On the eastern walkway of the Quay, voices bubble in the restaurants, queues form for party boats at the dock, light blazes. Amid the restaurants is a cinema, under renovation. 'I often come to this cinema even though there are others much closer, because I like to come out of the darkness into this space.' Dazzling to emerge here, to leave the place of memory and imagination, those images of far places, into the light and noise of this place, in this time. 'Roland Barthes talks about that lapse of time, coming out of the darkness, as if out of hypnosis. And Italo Calvino writes in his memoir of seeing films in the daytime and emerging to discover it's night, that the whole world has changed while he's been suspended in space.'

Light pours down on the gleaming Opera House and the broad forecourt. Rounding Bennelong Point, gazing up at the reflections of water and walkers in the glazed façades, Gail gestures towards another *Five Bells*: John Olsen's glowing indigo painting with its spots and squiggles of light and memory, kept behind curtains, 'only revealed at night'. Olsen has written of it: 'That blue luminescence in the mural is the equivalent of water on the harbour, the phosphorescence ... the feeling of flying over Sydney Harbour but also sinking beneath the sea.' Gail refers to early lines of the Slessor poem, the 'deep and dissolving verticals of light' that 'ferry the falls of moonshine down'. What attracts her is 'the vertical movement into deep self: into memory and into consciousness, the fine-tuning of perception to the outside. It's very encouraging as a writer to think about that, to think about how beautiful it is.'

Here on Bennelong Point, or Djubuguli, we are on a former tidal island. All around the Quay, and many shores of the harbour, colonial claims reengineer the shoreline. 'There's a sign in front of Customs House that says this is where the shoreline used to be. At that end of Circular Quay it was mudflats – the hotels are on pylons thirty metres deep in the mud across the Tank Stream.' Such a loss, that the city's first water source is buried beneath buildings. There is a lottery; on dry days lucky winners head down into a tunnel beneath Pitt Street to walk through the stormwater drain, once a fresh stream upon which to build a colony. Development unearths remnants of time past. The works for the Metro, excavating under Central Station, revealed colonial graves. Beneath this city, we are reminded, is another, many others.

Heading back towards the Royal Botanic Garden along the eastern side of the Opera House, it feels as though time is set out grandly on a stage. Ahead is the ancient sandstone of the Botanic Garden, sliced into a platform wall: 'When I first came to Sydney, I was so struck by these walls of stone: the colour, the palette, the way they change colour with water.' The flank of the Opera House curves above, its tessellated tiles in intricate pattern. Up at the Garden as you round the point is the gleaming sculpture *bara*, by Waanyi artist Judy Watson – a monumental fishhook like those used by Gadigal women on these waters.

Tucked away just south of the Quay on Bridge Street are the remnants of the first NSW Governor's house beneath the Museum of Sydney. 'Something that I think about in relation to the deep time here is that Barangaroo and Arabanoo were both buried in the governor's garden. There's nothing to mark that, and there's no visible sense of what was there before. You have the cadastral city, the city mapped out by the colonists, according to grids, property borders, and the straightness of roads. Then you have the topography; you have the tracks made by Aboriginal people with bare feet walking down to the water. You have stories. You have all these adjacencies in time that aren't visible now.' In the Indigenous concept of everywhen, all times are present. Glimpsing such knowledge, for we latecomers, 'invests things with a secret perpetuity'.

Here in this moment, *here-now* – a refrain in Gail's *Five Bells* – the water sucks against the sandstone walls. A train rumbles into the elevated station. Cranes squeak as they swing loads of dirt. Time, as Slessor insisted, is not measured by 'fidget wheels'.

'There's a time in consciousness,' Gail says, 'there's a time in the earth, a time in the stars. There's time in quantum physics. None of this has anything to do with the "fidget wheels" of time, with the "bumpkin calculus".' How to access the presences in our city, the realities that precede us, the stories that lie out of sight? 'Walter Benjamin says that we have to wake back into the dream: waking up, as well as the "wake" of mourning what's not there, is an obligation of being alive, of being lucky to be here – the adventure of it. Why wouldn't you want to make the most of it, to share that with other people as ways of seeing?'

PARRAMATTA WILL NEVER BE COMPLETE

PARRAMATTA

WITH
EDA GUNAYDIN

All along the river new housing was being built, boutique hotels as well as serviced apartments. Western Sydney University's Parramatta campus had been erected, as if overnight, while I was gone, and its red logo drew the eye like a laser pointer. When I started attending workshops at nearby high schools, the students of a local school had been moved to a temporary campus, and were being taught out of demountables connected by wobbly, plastic ramps, which, a teacher informed me, had been thrown up in two months. The school was set to reopen as a high-rise. One of the students isn't taking it well, she remarked. He likes to go outside and let his feet touch the ground on occasion, feel the grass – it helps him think.

– Eda Gunaydin, 'Second City'

Parramatta, as much as anywhere in Sydney, demonstrates the dizzying pace of change this city can impose upon its people. This 'second city' contains both the oldest colonial building in Australia and, at any given moment, various examples of the newest, its streetscapes and skyline constantly under re-formation. In the vivid green park on the river, sitting on the slope of lawn leading up to Old Government House, you can hear the mad squawking of cockatoos and the low rumble of traffic and construction while high-rises bloom skyward above the trees. Here you are on the site of the first government farm, land stolen swiftly after the arrival of the First Fleet in Sydney Cove for the feeding of the starving colony.

Nourishing the lushness of this green place is the Parramatta River, winding westwards from the harbour, narrowing as it runs along between mangrove-lined banks. It is Parramatta's most ancient way, for millennia traversed, swum and fished by the Burramattagal, a clan of the Dharug people. The eels swam from the coast to these waters to breed, sustaining the Burramattagal and giving the clan, and the modern city, their name.

Parramatta is generally known as the largest urban centre in Western Sydney, though on a map, and in its demographic mix, it lies at Sydney's heart. In her essay 'Second City', an account of leaving and returning to Parramatta, Turkish-Australian writer and researcher Eda Gunaydin examines the complexities of gentrification, of self and of this place. In her work more generally she writes often about the materiality of living in Western Sydney, a huge area with varied and complex meanings:

> I am loath to think of it as a place with a fixed geography ... it would be more appropriate to call it a constellation of social meanings stitched together and imputed on an ever-warping set of geographies, with Western Sydney emerging as whatever the centre discards in its periphery.

The collection in which these reflections appear, *Root & Branch: Essays on Inheritance*, explores the legacies of migration and class with political acumen and a self-deprecating wit. Another of the enjoyable textures of Eda's writing is the presence on the page of untranslated Turkish. Outsiders must read actively, phone in hand, scraping at the layers of story and language, seeking glimpses of meaning and suggestion. This reading experience is something like a walk with Eda: here is the surface of things; engage further and your curiosity will be both rewarded and further piqued.

Eda grew up in Blacktown, a fifteen-minute train ride away; as she recounts in 'Second City', 'Paramatta has often felt like home ground to me ... a prime spot for shopping, socialising, picnics and nights out.' It is a place where her dad, on drives around the neighbourhood, pointed out houses he had worked on as a builder, and where her own history of work begins, tutoring at the library as a teenager and then, at a restaurant on Church Street, tolerating long, hot shifts of 'sustained smiling' and total physical exhaustion:

> I wrote some of these mundane details into short stories later: the kebab shop employee who has to rest her legs perpendicular up her wall so the swelling in her feet will come down; the young woman who sucks on olives while hidden in the kitchen in order to mainline herself enough salt and fat to make it through the day.

At the epicentre of the changing city is Parramatta Square, a place where social mobility takes built form. Brand-new towers line a pleasantly bustling square where office and construction workers, students and families mill about between the restaurants, and kids bounce on and off the street furniture. St John's Anglican Cathedral is a reminder of the scale of times past, a miniature sandstone remnant amid the mirrored towers. Eda points out a local detail: a cluster of police officers watching the comings and goings from one end of the square. What she notices 'about stepping off the train at Parramatta is this police presence, even going through the ticket gates. For me, coming from the inner west and having grown up in Western Sydney, it's always notable.'

Halfway along the square, at number 5, is the new library and cultural space, PHIVE, with its red-and-orange roof curving up and away, suggesting a Chinese tiled roof in its tessellated form and swoop. This generous and distinctive building is nevertheless small and Lego-ish amid the towers. Behind it is a city block–sized construction zone emitting a Parramatta soundtrack of grinding and beeping, bobcats crawling across the mounds of dirt. All this digging cannot help but unearth the past. Not long ago, the PHIVE site was excavated and Eda learned that there were two layers of discovery beneath the surface. 'There's a lot of recovered material from Parramatta's colonial past – crockery and porcelainware – but underneath that they recovered middens that attest to the Aboriginal coastal use of the area. The things that were recovered are now being held in this very building, in a cultural keeping space.' This space, which you can make an appointment to visit, houses these items along with those returned to Country from other institutions.

The foyer of the library is calm and welcoming, open to the square and to anyone who wants to sit down for a while out of the elements. Families pass through with purposeful cheer on their way to the books and activities. Light floods in through the walls of windows, even on an overcast day. The old Parramatta Library, the site of Eda's teenage tutoring job with students of local high schools, has gone now, moved to make way for the development of Parramatta Square. Downstairs in the new library are spaces where cultural events take place, part of the 'large arts and entertainment push' in the area. Eda, as part of an arts group called Finishing School Collective, helps to organise events here and across Sydney that consider Western Sydney as place and idea. Not long after this walk, the collective transforms a large, blank underground room in the building into a space of stories, poems, food and connection;

in it, writers tell of life in this city – of family, diaspora, queerness – with a rich sense of its multiplicity.

There's a pause before leaving the library, as Eda adjusts her mental map to navigate the new reality of the re-formed square. It is easy to think that one day the change will finish, your bearings will settle and your personal geography will be re-fixed, just as soon as the streets have finished morphing around you. Eda recently wrote an essay for a photography project by the artist Cherine Fahd called *Being Together: Parramatta Yearbook*. 'It was a reflection on a changing city. She set up large sets in a few iconic parts of Parramatta and asked passers-by to pose for photographs.' After months of lockdown and curfews, Fahd captured building crews, kids, the 'Women's Shed', football fans, nurses – everyone – as they emerged back onto the streets. Many of them smile warmly in Fahd's photographs, behind them building sites, the new stadium, the ordinary daily places of Parramatta in flux. The photos were displayed in an outdoor installation at Centenary Square so that the community could see themselves and the people they knew as they walked by. In Eda's essay, she brings to life the 'pounding and banging of construction that underscores every moment one spends outside', 'the mash of bodies on Church Street' on match days, 'the relentless hum of people moving in and out'. She spoke to people involved in the project, and to heritage workers, considering 'the human and cultural cost of "development"'. In her conversations, she says, 'the most interesting reflection I heard was that Parramatta, like any other city, will never be complete'.

Bearings straight, we head east past the new high-rise campus of Western Sydney University, where Eda worked for a while as an editor at the *Sydney Review of Books*, a hothouse of contemporary writing from and on Western Sydney and further afield; the journal's offices were the site of Eda's book launch for her essay collection *Root & Branch*. The new urban towers of the university are springing up across Western Sydney, here and in Bankstown and Liverpool, bringing new flows of people and energy through these civic centres.

Across Smith Street from Parramatta Square is Lancer Barracks, the oldest army barracks in continual use in mainland Australia, built to house British regiments enforcing the rule of law upon the convict colony and to combat Aboriginal resistance, which was fierce in Parramatta. These colonial buildings are in good shape: well-maintained examples of early Australian architecture. Standing outside the locked front fence of the barracks, if you turn in a circle you see buildings from a dizzying number of eras from the past two centuries or so. 'This mix of architecture is fairly typical of Sydney. You've got a couple of things that might be old but from different periods, with very new buildings dwarfing them.'

Next door is the playing field of Arthur Phillip High School, whose students Eda has tutored, and the first public high-rise school in New South Wales. In a news article about the new school building, a spokesperson for the Department of Education was quoted as saying, 'The abseiling window cleaners, we're going to have to get kids used to that.' It is valuable to provide public-school children with modern amenities, but the changes take a bit of adjustment. Eda talks about 'mental geography' in her writing to describe the complex and dynamic overlays of memory and place. Streets disappear; a school shoots up into the sky from its broad green field. 'That's partially why I have such new difficulty navigating this suburb. My mental geography of this place is based on historical layering. All this seems to represent the next layer that I'm still coming to terms with.' In Rebecca Solnit's writing on the flâneurs of Paris, she recounts how, in the mid-nineteenth century, 'the old Paris was cut down like a forest' by the architect Baron Haussmann. 'In tearing down so much of the old city, he obliterated the delicate interlace of mind and architecture, the mental map walkers carried with them and the geographical correlatives to their memories and associations.' Eda works to process such change through how it 'maps onto my own personal biography, how I interact with Parramatta as my jobs and social class have changed over the years'.

Macquarie Street is blocked off, for now, for the construction of the new Metro station, so to travel westwards towards the parklands we have to first walk north along Smith Street to George. On the corner, in a Victorian sandstone building, is Story Factory, an organisation founded in Redfern that provides writing workshops for schoolchildren. In the last fifteen or so years, there have been a number of arts initiatives for young people in Western Sydney, amid a broader upsurge of writing and art of the area coming to national attention. One such organisation, WestWords, brought Eda back to the area for work, where she hoped to make a difference in the community in which she grew up. In 'Second City', Eda navigates the tension between material conditions and the important provision of opportunities and encouragement:

> there were young people of colour in Western Sydney, like me, who needed to be told that their stories were important and that they shouldn't be ashamed to tell them, that they could write and that they needn't stage their work in Parisian apartments or English meadows they had never visited.

She finds, after some months in the role, that the problems of access to the arts have not disappeared since she worked long hours in a restaurant: that time and money and knowledge of available programs still grant a considerable edge. 'I should have known this,' she writes. It was only after the years of 'working my way into a comfortable position in life through brute force' that 'the words burbled up'.

Almost opposite Story Factory, at the edge of the hollowed-out block being dug up for the Metro station, sits the Roxy Theatre in grubby, isolated splendour. Built in the Spanish Baroque style in 1930 and subject of a campaign to restore it to its former glory, it is currently blocked by an ugly gate, flanked on one side by a takeaway, and miniaturised by the empty block and towers behind it. The back of PHIVE's roof glows amid the grey buildings across the dusty building yard. Various plans have been floated for the theatre, election promises made. There are attractive pictures online linking it to a grassy plaza and Parramatta Square, the Metro right next door. For now the outlook for this distinctive building is uncertain. 'When I was researching the Roxy it was my understanding that it was about to be taken over for business purposes. They tried to create an arcade feel here with some restaurants. It could be a music venue – if you want to see live music in Sydney, you have to go to the inner west. It's a real shame about the Roxy.'

At the end of the block is Church Street, lined with restaurants, once a noisy evening parade of throatily powerful cars, now blocked off to traffic for the construction of the light rail. The street is a mix: chain restaurants like Betty's Burgers, local restaurants, a gym, vape shops, gaps where businesses have closed. Here's the restaurant of Eda's youth, hopefully gentler on its workers these days. Peering in at the walls lined with pictures as we pass by she says, 'If you look closely, one of the photographs is the owner. I used to have to dust the tops of the frames.' Church Street is loud, currently, even without the traffic, music blaring, building work rumbling away in the blocks around. 'You used to be able to smoke here. There were lots of shoeshine establishments, for better or worse. The street used to be fairly vibrant. From my understanding it's been quite difficult to reactivate this area post-lockdown because the construction traffic is now also atrocious. It's impossible to park here, not just because of the light rail clearances, but also because of the recently completed stadium, any time there's a game on.' The street is between phases, and yet on a Ramadan evening at around this time, it is alive with families making the most of the lull between cars and the tram, sitting on temporary structures in the street. People queue out of the restaurants and a New Orleans–style trio marches up and down Church Street and across Lennox Bridge and back. In the evening, when the construction rests, the people of Parramatta make a more festive sound than the machinery ever-present in the day.

As Church Street reaches the river, the noise falls away. After rain, the water is murky, but there are lovely old trees, and a flying fox colony further along the river. 'When the flying foxes make their way out at sunset it's very beautiful.' The paths through the parklands are good for cycling and walking, but the river is not swimmable, its industrial past yet to be remediated. 'There's an old gasworks where coal would come down the river, and a gas light company was established when lighting became the craze. There's been significant industrial pollution, the effects of which are still being felt.'

Standing on Lennox Bridge – one of New South Wales' oldest and quarried from sandstone at the Parramatta Female Factory – you can see the building site of the new Powerhouse Museum where it stretches along the south bank of the river.

The Powerhouse has recently published a collection of stories – *The River* – about this waterway: its cultural significance and history, its mangroves, rituals and soundscapes. In one of these pieces, Willem Brussen, a descendant of the Baramadagal of the Dharug nation, speaks to Dharug elders about the ways in which the river tells the story of the Baramadagal Country that goes back thousands of years. They discuss trees growing into concrete and fencing, which can be seen as a metaphor for colonialism: 'Country bears the scars of its people,' Brussen writes:

> Where the ferry comes in now, a little further east from Lennox Bridge, the clans gathered to feast on eels. To the west, the warrior Pemulwuy fought the Battle of Parramatta, where he was shot but escaped. The river brings sadness but also hope for the people to whom it has long had meaning.

Brussen concludes that 'like the river that still flows, we are still here'.

Down on the riverbank, next to the new sandstone wall of a commercial building, is a collection of supermarket trolleys, arranged upside down in an arty formation. To the east, the path is broken by the construction works of the new Powerhouse building. Across the river the Riverside Theatres take out a section of riverfront. To their west the riverside path resumes, a glowing green playing field stretching away, beautiful little kids running everywhere. Behind the field sits a symmetrical row of stately colonial buildings, at their centre a slab of sandstone grandeur, the Old King's School, part of the original government farm. Now it is Bayanami Public School; beyond it looms the new football stadium. You can imagine the roar at the weekend, the traffic chaos, the streams of people walking in the same direction.

Passing beneath a brutalist concrete bridge, you emerge to a view of the stadium, a carpark, new apartments and the green floodplain of the park. This area is the site of the colony's first farm, established in November 1788 in the area they named Rosehill. A sign says that 'the undulating, fertile land that attracted the European settlers was the result of Aboriginal Land Management methods', a polite reference to the brazen theft of land so beautifully cared for. The cockatoos are raucous, deafening, claiming the land and sky.

Part of Eda's work with WestWords was producing the Parracons Poetry Trail, an interactive collection of student and published poetry responding to important places in Parramatta. While researching the locations, she found herself

> stopped in the middle of Parramatta Park, feet blistered and aching from my office sandals. I stood holding up a piece of paper I had printed out from a study documenting the various trees in the park, some of which still bore visible 'scars'. These were markings from sections of the tree which had had their bark stripped away by the Burramatta people of the Dharug nation, to build canoes.

Looking at these trees, the layers of time are all around, in the green floodplain, beneath the looming stadium, the cranes of Parramatta beyond the park. 'What I find confronting about the trees is that you get a sense of just how recently this place was colonised. It really is not very long ago, especially thinking about other settler-colonial contexts. Parramatta has some of the oldest colonial history in New South Wales and it's still not particularly old.'

Across the park, pretty but imposing on the rise of the hill, is Old Government House, built by John Hunter; it is Australia's oldest public colonial building. The commanding position of the house 'shows what kind of chokehold this area was under in terms of colonial presence and enforcement'. From those early days of the colony in Parramatta there were also the women and girls at the Female Factory, 'serving time for attempting to escape and other infractions. It makes me think about the police and the militarised presence here. I feel that presence has never gone away.' This kind of presence was tangibly felt during the pandemic when the phrase 'LGAs of concern' echoed across the Sydney airwaves in reference to the cluster of Western Sydney council areas placed under special restrictions and curfews, causing intense difficulty and often resentment. It was a time when, as Eda puts it, 'states of exception' were applied, the usual rule of law suspended in response to a particular event. A reminder of the presence of such authority in people's lives is the courts, at the eastern end of the park, across O'Connell Street. 'These courts are a big part of what brings people commuting into Parramatta.' Here, within a minute or two's walk of one another, are the Federal Circuit and Family Court, Children's Court, District Court, Local Court, the Department of Communities and Justice and the police station, many of the offices crammed between them occupied by lawyers.

Back on Church Street, at Centenary Square, the early colonial St John's Cathedral and the pretty town hall are dwarfed by the immense 6&8 Parramatta Square buildings. Along the wall here is where the photographs from Cherine Fahd's *Parramatta Yearbook* were displayed, the people of Parramatta looking back at themselves as they went about their business. There were table-tennis tables here too, another gathering point for the people of Parramatta. Around the corner in Parramatta Square the tables remain, as well as a large chessboard, where men gather and contemplate the scenario.

Eda says goodbye to head to the train station, but before she does, she sends me off to the Female Factory precinct, beyond the stadium on the eastern side of the river as it wends north. It is an important site in Parramatta, where the themes of this walk – control, culture, memory – come together in one eerily beautiful place. The large sandstone structures of the Female Factory, the Lunatic Asylum, Roman Catholic Orphan School and Parramatta Girls Home are silent except for the squawking of flying foxes at the colony on the river. Thousands of girls and women suffered here during almost the entire span of the colony, the former Girls Home operating as a women's prison until 2011. It is hard to know what to feel as you walk among the buildings, imagining what sounds you might have once heard. Eda told me of the ghost tours and movie screenings put on in this place, its development as an arts precinct, and the pushback against using such sites for entertainment. The Parragirls, a group of women previously incarcerated at the site, fought for years to make public the brutal history of these institutions. In 2017 they gained a national heritage listing for the precinct, making it a 'site of conscience', a historic site that resists the erasure of its violent past. Here, as elsewhere in Parramatta, the past makes itself felt, but it is its people who insist that we look, and reflect, rather than walk on by.

SLIPPING INTO THE CURRENT

KING STREET, NEWTOWN

WITH VANESSA BERRY

> I first visited King Street as a teenager. I'd try on secondhand clothes at The Look or go to the night markets in Burland Community Hall, or just watch the people a little older than me, goths and punks, people with bright hair and weird clothes, whose lives I hoped to emulate ... Despite the fact many had come before me, I felt that King Street and the inner west was the home that I had chosen, rather than the home I was born into.
>
> – Vanessa Berry, 'Newtown in the 1990s Map'

King Street, Newtown, in the inner west of Sydney, is a grittily attractive street of legend and memory as well as a grinding thoroughfare threaded between faded, colourful Victorian and early twentieth-century terraces, theatres and shops that are beautifully, often scruffily intact. These buildings, sprouting with ferns and decorated with exuberant graffiti, are the backdrop to meandering daytime trawls of the book, antique and op shops and nights out at the restaurants, bars and old-school pubs. The streetscape has survived because the neighbourhood was considered too impoverished to bother developing, and this once-cheap, still-beautiful housing has generated an artistic and alternative cultural history continually drawing waves of young people who renew the area's energies.

Denizen of the inner west Vanessa Berry is known for her zines, essays, blogs, talks and books on the pleasures of underground worlds, and of the secret city that offers glimpses of the arcane to the curious. She has an affinity for the neglected surfaces and remnants that give places like Newtown an enchantment that is always in and out of time. Her memoir *Ninety9* tells the story of a suburban teenager drawn by the magnetism of '90s music and alternative culture to Newtown and Glebe. Here a young goth adventurer could browse the shops, trawl the night markets looking for special trinkets, find her tribe. In Vanessa's *Mirror Sydney* blog, a hand-drawn map of Newtown offers access to her memories and an invitation to readers to share their own, to explore and imagine what the old signs mean, what a curious window display might offer.

A walk from one end of King Street to the other takes you along a stretch of the Princes Highway from the University of Sydney through the heart of Newtown to St Peters and Sydney Park in the south: just over two kilometres of Victorian façades, traffic noise, graffiti and interesting people to consider and enjoy. From the city end of the street, Vanessa points out its alluring shape: 'There are a few curves to it that make it quite an exciting street to walk along, topographically. It has these phases where you can't quite see all the way from beginning to end, and in my many walks along King Street over the years, that's always been part of the experience.' The first milestone of the King Street wander is the building which from 1989 to 2018 housed Gould's Book Arcade. The freestanding, triple-fronted former home of 'James Castle & Sons Art Metal Workers' reveals its history in intriguing layers. Mastheads of newspapers line the awning, and underneath, protected from sun and rain, the painted sign 'Gould's Books & Video: Records • Cassettes • CD's bought & sold' is as sharp as ever. Ancient movie posters, some just legible – *A Clockwork Orange*, *Return to Oz* – flap under the awning of the locked-up building. The ruined paper has an unnerving texture, clumped, organic, lines of text visible in places, areas that look burned.

'When I walk down King Street, it's always walking through a number of different times and selves all at once. Many who gravitate to Newtown remember when they first came here. For me, that was the 1990s. Gould's was in full swing by then; it opened here in 1989. It seemed like it had been there forever.' The shop was a chaotic cavern of thousands of books, magazines and videos; finding what you wanted came down to serendipity. It lured you in to wander, lost and beguiled, among the aroma of sweetly decomposing old books. 'It was a place to go if there was nowhere else to go, and there'd always be someone walking in and saying "Whoa, look at all the books!" They were encountering it for the first time. I loved that about it.'

Bob Gould, early opponent of the Vietnam War and gruff and committed socialist, ran his shop on this site for thirty years, until his death from falling down the stairs while stacking books. The business lives on in King Street, at the south end, in a smaller, tidier form, run by Bob's daughter Natalie. When it became clear the bookshop could not hang on in its large building against rising rents, people's love and memories poured forth, in the press, on social media, in conversations between Newtown residents past and present. 'Something happens as certain shops become more than a commercial enterprise in people's minds. They become a community place as well. You're losing a place where you could go and feel connected with a world, or a subculture.'

The right-hand side, as you walk away from the city, is Vanessa's preferred side. Crossing the busy street towards it, in the window of a business a yellow sign reads 'Cordobes'. It's from a former pizza restaurant, 'Alex Cordobe's – a good little pizza place that had lots of paintings of birds inside. It was very atmospheric, one of those places I can walk back into in my memory really strongly, because it had a distinct mood.' It's a Pilates studio now, 'we're at that stage in gentrification. But I love it that they put up the sign.'

King Street likes to acknowledge its own heritage; it's part of its distinctive texture in a city whose streetscapes are rapidly changing. From around the 1960s, when Newtown's student and countercultural life began, the sense of the past has been part of the draw: 'people come here for that experience of patina and layers'. Next door to the Cordobes building, at 69–77 King Street, is an ornate Flemish-style building, once the Trocadero, established in 1889 in a moment of boom-time enthusiasm for indoor rollerskating. Like many of the buildings on this strip, it has witnessed within its walls a dramatic array of experience. Little wheels no longer glide across its floor, but it has in its time housed a coach-builder, vaudeville shows, amateur boxing and a mechanic's shop.

Above the shopfronts, plants creep from the walls like a reclamation: 'Ah, the hardy ferns – King Street has a different kind of world above the awning.' Up there, as well as the ferns there is graffiti, and often people, watching the world pass by beneath. 'How cool do you feel sitting above King Street? Especially if you're in a share house, or you're a younger person. It is one of those places where people feel a strong sense of connection. This is their place – they have chosen it – often people who come here because they don't feel particularly welcome where they grew up.'

The intersection with Missenden Road is dominated by the Art Deco Marlborough Hotel, site of another community outpouring when they replaced the old tiles with the gleaming white façade of today, and here too is the treasure trove of Vinnies, a bit tidy these days for Vanessa but still holding promise. The processes of searching and salvaging in op shops, for her, is related to writing. In her essay 'The Writer's Clutter', she says of her migrations to these stores:

I felt drawn to placing myself among these discards, to search and to salvage. Writing and op-shopping became intertwined activities. I'd sit on a train, travelling through the Sydney suburbs, going as far and visiting as many op shops as it took to unlock my thoughts ... to find within the ordinary matter of life, the details, moments or objects that can speak of deeper things.

The shops here have a social aspect. You can wander down King Street with friends, or run into people you know. In the old days you might start at Gould's, have a wander round Vinnies, stop at a cafe or one of the pubs. People have their 'circuits', and their versions of this place in its past and its present. 'I'm very conscious when I write about places that I have a version of, that many people have other versions, and to let them all exist at once.' Visits to this part of Sydney as a teenager brought 'a sense of space and freedom. I wasn't being surveilled. I could just work things out for myself. Newtown felt like a space where that could happen, and it still does. Especially on the weekends, kids come in and they're often styled in an alternative way. They find this same quality in the place that I found many years ago.'

Level with another of King Street's pubs, Coopers Hotel, the upper storeys of the streetscape opposite once more draw the gaze upwards. Above the chain restaurant Fishbowl, a strikingly modern building with a geometric, corrugated frontage is squeezed between the ornate old façades. 'When you're on King Street, you're very focused on street level, but it really rewards you stopping and looking above the street. I'll be on the bus reading, and I can look up and at any moment I know where I am because I recognise, say, the pink building with the columns and the garland of flowers and fruit on the top. It's one of those places that's patterned into my being.'

There are different speeds and modes at which one can take in King Street. On the bus, the street has 'a cinematic element, like a film going past the window'. When you're on wheels or tracks, the smoothness of the city passing by has that filmed quality. But walking can have an appealing flow too: 'Sometimes when I'm walking home, and I'm not stopping anywhere, I like cutting through the crowd, trying to keep up momentum. I love that feeling of moving among people. You know a place well and you know how to move there, and you can slip into its current. It's me doing the moving but it doesn't a hundred per cent feel that way.'

Turning off down Church Street, with its sweet cottages, towards St Stephen's Anglican Church and the graveyard, everything is suddenly quiet. Violence and threat seem far, but the cemetery behind the church was completely reshaped by the murder between the headstones of an eleven-year-old girl, Joan Norma Ginn, in 1946. The derelict graveyard, which used to stretch out into what is now a grassy park, was moved into the small area next to the church in an effort to clamp down on undesirable behaviour. Now this place has become a haven for the goth kids traipsing up and down King Street, a place out of sight, to relax and find your people.

King Street feels a million miles away as you pass into the shade of an enormous fig tree just inside the graveyard. Bees buzz at a cluster of hives, bamboo burgeons. This place has its own atmosphere, created through outsized greenery, overgrown grass, jumbled and crumbling sandstone gravestones – many lining the wall, brought in from the larger cemetery – and softly worn paths made by feet rather than concrete. The graves of those lost in the 1857 wreck of the *Dunbar* are here, marked by the ship's large anchor, and the resting place of Eliza Donnithorne, 'said to be the model for Dickens'

Miss Havisham'. There's a resistance to the smartening-up pressures of contemporary life that's part of the appeal of Newtown, its refusal to entirely succumb to gentility. The other side of the wall that sections off the cemetery is bright with graffiti. Over there, it 'has a different kind of atmosphere again, especially on the weekends. Everyone's out having picnics and it looks like a Richard Scarry picture – everyone's doing an activity': playing with dogs, sitting on a blanket, throwing a frisbee.

Back up on King Street, Elizabeth's Bookshop bustles with students, as it has for decades. Soon you reach the small courtyard in front of the *I Have a Dream* mural, painted illegally by Juilee Pryor and Andrew Aiken over two weekend nights in 1991, and heritage-listed in 2014. It has become another of Newtown's symbols of community, and has survived commercial interests and even fire. Pryor said of the painting: 'This was our gift to Newtown ... What we were looking for was a way to bring light.' The mural is accompanied by a smaller Aboriginal artwork to its right, which says, 'Smile, you're on Gadigal land'; it incorporates an Aboriginal flag, added since the original painting of the work.

Above the mural are small windows, leading you to imagine who might live behind these locally famous artworks. 'I always look at the apartments above when I'm on the other side of the road because it looks like a big old share house. I'd think, "Who lives there?"' Vanessa writes of her evening walks, and the everyday mystery of seeing briefly into the lives of others:

> when I go walking I can see into the rooms of the houses I pass by. At this time of day the lights are on inside but people have not yet drawn the curtains, providing a view to the rooms within. Sometimes I will see a person sitting hunched over a laptop, but often there is no one and my

eyes are free to roam over the details of the interior. The sofas, bookcases and dining tables have the expectant mood of stage sets.

Here too in the evenings, the huge windows of these apartments on King Street glow with possibility, the walls filled with posters, the suggestion of lives impressing themselves upon those who glance upwards for an instant from the busy street below.

This phase of King Street has remained largely unchanged for decades: the incense smell and alluring jumble of Eastern Flair, the inviting calm of the florist and Better Read Than Dead bookshop. The Oxford Tavern no longer occupies its corner: Vanessa has coasters from this pub with her friends' stories written on the back, 'like an artefact'. At the broad intersection of King Street and Enmore Road sits the Hub, the old 'adult cinema' that has been closed for decades, emitting the eternal Sydney mystery of how there can be enough spare money in the world for such a large building to sit idle. Of late a happy rumour is about that it has been sold to be used as a queer performance space. A plane passes over so low it almost skims the roofs of the buildings. Vanessa calls this section of King Street 'the split'. 'It's an important King Street moment, because it really changes in the south section – it feels just a little bit quieter. It becomes more minor. For a long time, there used to be the flowers that were painted in Reclaim the Streets in around 2000 on that traffic island there. I'd look for them whenever I'd go past.' In her blog post 'Newtown in the 1990s Map', there's a picture of her cheerfully reclaiming the streets, out in the middle of what is usually a murderous intersection.

Walking along south King Street, the buildings are smaller scale; there's more sky, and it's possible to talk without shouting.

A famous Newtown pub, the Sando, has suffered various indignities since the days when it launched a thousand bands, bouncing around on the makeshift stage inches from the bar staff. Until recently it was Holey Moley, a miniature golf course. For now, the façade of the empty building is still lined with pub tiles and the top half of the neglected Art Deco building bears the sign of the Sandringham Hotel.

Behind the old pub, we take a small detour off King Street to share a stickybeak at a house I lived in when I first moved to Sydney. Bold street art illuminates the end of a building – magpies with red eyes. Down the lane are graffitied garages, cute cottages. It's a dramatically different atmosphere to that on King Street: 'All of a sudden, the sound gets drawn away.' The house itself is typical of the area, a shabby, romantic terrace, its yellow paint flaking, its stone front step dipping from the tread of a century or so of feet, the metal doorbell, the alarming cracks in the plaster. Shaggy twin palms shoot up past the iron lace balcony. 'It's a very familiar kind of house. I think of all the houses like this that I went to for parties, or that my friends lived in. You'll walk in past the iron fence – if I close my eyes, I can almost just walk in and be there, just by looking at the outside.' Not long before, the house had been for sale, and it was permitted to have a poke around the once-grand old rooms. What's inside now are the Victorian tiles and pressed-metal ceilings and fireplaces of old, but also mould spreading like maps across the walls, kitchen floorboards spongy and dangerous. Memories of parties flicker in the dark rooms.

Back on King Street, this southern stretch still has a good selection of junk shops, with their familiar aesthetic of old magazines, stepped bookcases and incense collections, and shops with interesting displays. Vanessa explores the 'museum aspect' of certain stores in the inner west in her book

Mirror Sydney. The essay 'Memorial Stores' is named for the curious shop windows commemorating former businesses in Enmore and Ashfield. In that essay Vanessa writes too of the 'time-capsule stores' on Parramatta Road, which 'exist within their own bubble of time'; to pass inside is to leave the busy everyday world of the street and enter a different atmosphere. Here in Newtown, thriving businesses contribute their own intriguing displays to the interest of the street; we linger for a moment to examine the window of a popular photograph-developing place at 457, in which a funny little bear sits on a camera.

Walking down south King Street, the neighbourhood feels both more relaxed and more neglected than the busy stretch further north. Across the road, two big men with shaved heads and scruffy clothes run into each other. One is completely covered in tattoos and holds a tiny creature, a puppy the size of a kitten. The intimidating-looking men fuss over the little dog, a tenderness between them. Vanessa issues the gentle imperative to 'look closely' at a row of three terraces on that side of the street: the graffiti, the smashed windows, and the part-collapse in progress at the end of the row. The tiles have slid off the roof and the awnings slipped from the balcony. The lacework is 'dipping'. The row is like an ice-cream cake melting from one end. 'One house used to have vinyl records in the front garden; they were hanging down from the tree like a mobile or a wind chime.'

Bookish memories and sites linger in this stretch, where rent has traditionally been cheaper. There was for a while a salon for writers reading their short stories called 'Penguin Plays Rough' in a flat above a convenience store, which the writer Pip Smith ran in her front room. There were poetry nights around too, and there still are across the inner west, such as the long-running poetry night 'Avant Gaga' at Sappho's on Glebe Point Road. Over on the eastern side of south King Street is the new Gould's, carrying on its legacy at 536 in a smaller, tidier, less overwhelming form. At 573, the cosy Garden Lounge (green walls, eclectic old furniture and signs, old books) has been a homey gathering space for literary events, which now continue at pop-up venues. At 632 is Parliament on King, a community-minded cafe stuffed with books – they're piled high in the glass wall above the doors. Now visible above the roofs is one of the chimneys of the brickworks in Sydney Park. When you do a King Street walk in the opposite direction, it's the sight of Sydney Tower that signals the approaching finish, these tall landmarks like 'bookends for the street'.

And then you step off the end of King Street and into a different atmosphere again: the intimidating intersection where the street becomes the Princes Highway, and Sydney Park Road stretches away to the east. It's one of those in-between zones in Sydney, where you pass from one accommodating site to another, moving quickly from the curiosities of the street towards the old brick chimneys and the green rise of Sydney Park, beautiful now, full of tracks and public art and a skate park and wetlands.

Once the park too was a forbidding place, a vast rubbish tip, and even when it was greened over, it was still windswept, bleak even. As Vanessa writes in her essay 'Excavating St Peters', this area has spaces, with its heavy traffic and warehouses, which can be 'unlovely, surreal, resistant to investigation'. And yet with her characteristic commitment to noticing and discovering she tells the story of its passage from turpentine and ironbark forest and marshland, its colonial excavation for the brickworks and use as a dump, to a 'post-industrial playground for the musicians and artists who inhabited the city's edge'. These brickworks evoke the memories of the park's underground vibe before it was prettified: 'punks' picnics, raves, gigs: some official, some not'.

That scene, of its time and place, has passed by, but its ghostly footprint inspires new ones. When Vanessa came here, people told her she'd missed its heyday. Later she realised that 'the 1990s in Newtown had a really distinct identity, as it also had in the '80s, and it has now. I felt sustained by the place. The networks of people, but also the buildings, the houses, the streets – they became so familiar, they felt mine.' In spite or because of the ways in which Newtown cherishes its past, new people come, forming their own memories and connections, their own sense of making a home in the city.

THE IDEA OF A BEACH

FRESHWATER

WITH MALCOLM KNOX

> A claw of sandstone clasps its jewels: surf club, ocean bath, open-air public shower, refoliated dunes, alpha to omega told by one smile of golden sand and a drenching of scents: salt, wrack, sandstone, Norfolk Island pine resin. Not just a beach, but the idea of a beach.
>
> – Malcolm Knox, *Bluebird*

In Sydney's ocean-side suburbs, the elements are there to be enjoyed and often weathered: the glare of the sun-glazed ocean, the evening blast of summer southerlies, the sideways rain and thumping surf of east coast lows. Steep hills, rugged headlands and unstoppable flows of water make much of the terrain hard to access, but in a city where people will do anything for a view, houses spore like ferns on the headlands.

The long string of beaches that forms the north-eastern boundary of Sydney features in several of the novels of author and journalist Malcolm Knox, in which class, competition and masculinity shape the mythologies of these suburbs for a cast of legends, has-beens and also-rans. His characters are cursed by flickers of glory, dreams of the past and the future, images of perfection. A recent novel, *Bluebird*, is set in a beach town of the same name, a fictionalised version of the dreamy blue bay of Freshwater. Here amiable wreck Gordon Grimes clings grimly to the 'old Bluebird' and is salvaged daily by submersion in its legendary waves. Freshwater is a fitting inspiration for such a tale: a secluded nook between headlands where weatherboard cottages and 1960s units offer an alluring glimpse of the past amid the slick mansions, redeveloped pub and ever-spreading RSL, up on the point.

The walk begins on this headland, where you can turn in a circle and take in the long sweep of Curl Curl and Manly, and below you to the south, the gorgeous little scoop of Freshwater. Behind you is a small bushland park where the originator of Freshwater's surfing legend, Hawaiian longboard surfer Duke Kahanamoku, rides a slab of sandstone up in the salty air. Down the cement stairs at the ocean baths, swimmers carve up and down beside the rock platform. From here the path leads towards the beach, skimming the washing surf. The air at the edge of Sydney, below the ferny cliff, smells of sand, seaweed, damp stone.

From out here behind the surf, the waves build hypnotically towards the shore, scattered with patient surfers: beyond them is a house on the face of the headland, nowhere near a street, clinging to the rock like the wild greenery that surrounds it. In *Bluebird*, the derelict protagonist Gordon occupies 'The Lodge', 'a gob of bleached driftwood and cement render thrown against the cliff face'. It's a house falling into the sea, day by day, in which Gordon measures the increasing slope of the living-room floor by timing the passage of a marble rolling from one end to the other. The real-life inspiration for this house is beautifully restored, a jewel of a place out there on the rocks, but was once the pile of sticks of the novel. For Malcolm, it was the only time he has written a story so directly inspired by place. 'It was born when I was sitting out in the water, day after day, surfing. I'd imagine what might have gone on in that house over time. It looked like a heap of driftwood just thrown together. It's more than halfway down the face of the headland – you need to walk up forty metres' worth of staircase to get to the street above. It can't have been easy to build or, by our standards, legal. I'm told it was built around the 1930s or 1940s. It's got a point-blank view over the beach – you could literally fall off the balcony and land in the water, but I'm here a lot and I would say it's occupied about one week a year.'

Such places, trophies in the property portfolios of the super-rich, tell a story of the dramatic gentrification of Freshwater. 'For younger people, it's so much more expensive than it was to live here now. The big change was underway before the 1990s. It had been a proper working-class area with tradies or people whose families had got in in the 1940s, when there was a lot of public housing and low-cost workers' housing. It was considered a pretty rough suburb. The pub up the road, known as the Harbord Hilton, was a bit of a bloodhouse. And then the RSL up on the hill was indicative of an older, mainly white demographic.'

Early in the twentieth century, the rowdy reputation of the suburb led to a name change. Clusters of shacks formed weekend holiday camps where young people from the city would come and make merry, enjoying the surf and freedom. Reports of swearing, arrests over a sly-grog shop in the back of a truck and even a shooting fuelled a push to shed the tarnished name of Freshwater. From 1923, for eighty-five years, the suburb was called Harbord, before residents asked for it to be changed back again. Crossing the beach, you can see some of the stages of the suburb's development: the yellow 1930s surf club at centre stage, the mid-century unit blocks dotted across the valley, the more recent clifftop mansions towering over the village.

Out on the bay, waiting for the next decent wave, 'there's all sorts. It's not yuppies and wealthy people sitting out there in the surf, particularly among the locals – meaning people who surf most days. The majority of them are people who've been here for many years. I don't know where a lot of them live, but certainly they haven't moved in recently.' Most surfers at this beach are male, in spite of the growth in women's surfing, and most are locals. 'The chat is about the last wave, the next wave, the board. It's surf talk. People are out there to share an obsession: that's their common ground. That's their language. I am definitely an outsider, because I've only lived here for fifteen years. I'm still a blow-in and I always will be.'

Standing on the sand, watching the surfers bob on the waves, it seems like there's all the space in the world on the wide blue ocean, but as with the real estate on land there is a hierarchy. 'The people sitting in the best spots are a mixture of the old pecking order and the young guns, between about sixteen and twenty-five, who can get into those spots because they're the fastest paddlers, the best surfers. They're the ones who can get very, very deep on the wave, into a difficult place to take off – and yet can also make the most of the wave. For those longer-term surfers and the better surfers, they read everything better than the less-experienced surfer. That's their chief qualification.'

In Malcolm's novel *The Life*, broken-down surfing legend DK recalls his early acculturation to surfing: watching the behaviour of waves from his classroom, swimming in the ocean, somehow missing the 'kook' or clumsy know-nothing stage: 'Been watching them waves so long I knew what to do first up. Had it sorted. Paddled like there was a school of great whites snapping at me toes. Paddle and commit.' DK reads the water, absorbing how to interact with its dynamics, how to time action and release energy to fit its movements. 'We often confuse intelligence with ability to articulate. If you learn surfing, like any sport, when you're very young, you've internalised all of those factors before you articulate them,' Malcolm says. 'By the time you're an adult, it's all just flow and sync. For somebody like me, who came to board riding as an adult, it's still quite conscious. It's something I'm able to articulate because I came to it later.'

At the southern corner of the beach, a path leads across the grass reserve to Undercliff Road, where the Harbord Hilton (officially the Harbord Hotel) occupies most of a block on the way up towards the shopping village. In *Bluebird*, the 'Bluebird Hilton' is mid-transformation from pokie-crammed money spinner to high-end accommodation. In real life, the transition from rowdy beer barn to hipster and family-friendly venue is complete. Behind the pub, Undercliff Road, becoming Bridge Road, climbs to the headland between Freshwater and Queenscliff. From up here you can see the other local institution, the surf club. In the novel, there is also the firehouse, and these places form nodes in the network around which Bluebird's residents drift and cluster. 'I was banking with that book on so many of these features of a beach being generic, not just generalisable across beaches, but also across other types of communities.' In *Bluebird*, for example, after a dramatic incident on the beach, the locals drift towards the pub, drawn to the place where they can speculate over a beer or two. 'Those people could find each of those locations in their sleep. That's the common factor I was looking for. That geography becomes their internal landscape.' There's something deeply known and felt about these gathering places, in fiction and in real life. The Harbord Hotel taps into this strain; on its website the pub is called Freshwater's 'shrine by the sea'.

Cresting the hill you pass into the small headland suburb of Queenscliff. The view down Bridge Road: a long stretch of Manly, lined with Norfolk Island pines, leading towards North Head. These rising astonishments as you reach the summit of a hill or turn a corner call to some old yearning, feeding local mythologies. 'There is something pseudo sacramental in the beach and in the worship of the beach. A lot of people who move here are people who've grown up in the suburbs, where the most precious memories of childhood, of weekends and public holidays, are the ritual of going to the beach. Since childhood, they've come back here – maybe they're trying to retrieve something – and that can often be allied with the feeling of danger. When you're a kid from the suburbs it's impressed on you how dangerous the surf is, how there are sharks out there and rips: all these ways to die. You don't often have that in Australian suburbia: that confrontation with danger and the overcoming of mortal fear. I think that's a kind of a substratum in everybody's experience of the beach: that during their lives, at some point, they've had to face and overcome the fear.'

In Malcolm's writing, the beach suburbs form a sunny overlay to more troubling kinds of knowledge, working their way into a local experience of place. 'There's another layer, familiar to people who spend their entire lives in beachside suburbs, and that's the history that accumulates of extremely sad events. The beaches in Sydney are a concentrated locale of suicides, drownings, and a history of bashings and murders of gay men. Those unsolved stories you hear about put a hook in you, because if they've happened at Manly Beach or Whale Beach, or Bondi Beach, or Maroubra, that's the Australia that we love and cherish.'

The point at Queenscliff is the end of a suburban street. The edge is precipitous; you are protected from a fall by nothing but your own caution. From here you can see the former St Patrick's Seminary presiding over the south end of Manly, 'the location of terrible things that happened within the Catholic Church, in one of the more idyllic locations in the world. How do you interpret the vision of St Patrick's, sitting up there, so beautiful and so proud, and yet also the site of secrets and darkness?'

On the way back towards the beach along Pavilion Street, an archway in a sandstone wall entices you into Freshwater

View Reserve where swathes of blue open up beyond this magical green space. At the edge of the headland, jackhammers compete with the boom of the waves; beyond the walls of the garden are what Malcolm refers to as 'the empty castles' – houses under constant renovation, elbowing each other aside for a slice of the view.

Vantage points like this offer not just a pretty outlook but a sense of what the waves are up to. In the carparks in *Bluebird*, and those scattered through the Sydney beach suburbs and all along the coast, regulars gather in a great range of ages, pondering the surf. From these high places, 'everything always looks more organised. From above, you can read the surf a lot more easily. The waves look bigger. You get a bit twitchy – it always looks better from above.' Observation of the waves can be a sport in itself. 'There's the bench of broken dreams down at Manly, populated by men who can't or don't surf anymore. They're still there, checking it out and talking about it. And even if they're just watching somebody else on a wave, that's what they love.'

Access to the beach is a deeply held democratic ideal in Australian culture: the right of old men to sit around on benches contemplating the conditions, of teenagers to get up to no good in the dunes, of toddlers to fill their cossies with sand until they're corralled into the beach shower. 'In a lot of places in the USA and Europe, you wouldn't have access to a beach like this. The entire waterfront would be taken up by private property. In Malibu, they have some of the most gorgeous beaches in the world – really nice surf breaks – but there's a four- or six-lane highway running along metres from the water, and between the highway and the water is house after house after house without any public access between. Private property has locked the beach away.' Australian beaches have been subjected to abusive treatment in the past too. Malcolm recalls holidays as a child on the NSW north coast where rutile, a mineral used in paint and plastics, was mined on the beaches. Blueys Beach, a spectacular long white beach near Forster, was the site of a 'stinking great mining rig churning, churning through the sand. All up and down the New South Wales coast there were rigs on our most beautiful beaches and that was normality in the seventies. For a good chunk of Australia's colonial history, the beaches were just seen as more natural resources to plunder.'

Down near Freshwater surf club there's a stone surfboard with two plaques set into it. They acknowledge the first people of the area and commemorate the establishment of Manly-Freshwater as first, in 2010, a National Surfing Reserve, and then two years later as a World Surfing Reserve. A 'World Surfing Reserve', the plaque explains, 'proactively identifies, designates and preserves outstanding waves, surf zones and their surrounding environments around the world.' The idea of what a beach means and is for has changed as our consciousness grows of the fragility, value and cultural meanings of the zone between land and sea.

Wandering back across the beach to the ocean pool track where the walk began, Malcolm ponders walking as an end in itself. 'I'll walk half an hour, if need be, with the surfboard to a wave, but I've lost the gift of just walking, as we have today, without any end in mind. I've lost the art.' Though, like many a writer, he walks his way out of difficulty. 'It's something I choose to do, if I'm having a moment of crisis. It's always beneficial.' Given the chance, writers will meander and idle, let the cogs shift, and Malcolm has moved his creative idling offshore: 'I spend quite a bit of time down here bobbing around in the water doing nothing.' We're back at the point across the bay from the house on the cliff that entered his imagination, releasing a story, as he waited for a wave.

As the walk comes to an end on this brightening morning, the talk turns – as it tends to do by the ocean – to weather: 'We've had the old four seasons, haven't we?' In *Bluebird*, moody days at the beach are Gordon's deep love, when he can surf on rainy days, gloriously alone, with an appreciation for the elements Malcolm shares. 'Surfing can be really beautiful in the middle of rain. Often in summer the weather can be unsettled, but when the rain hits, everything goes – the wind drops and everything is quite still – apart from the fact that a whole lot of water is being released from above you. When you're sitting in the surf and that happens, it's one of the times I love.'

TODAY

YAGOONA AND BANKSTOWN

WITH
SHEILA NGỌC PHẠM

Whenever I have touched on Western Sydney's history in my work, I try to centre the cultural richness and strength of communities; access to universal healthcare and education; selective schools; the role of public libraries; cultural spaces including places of gathering and worship; affordable higher education and universities. I name these specific factors because they all played important roles in my own development, however imperfectly, and a great many other people's as well. I'd like to think I'm an example of what's possible when we promote communitarian values and work hard to ensure justice, while honouring agency and the capacity of individuals to seek their own pathways to self transformation.

– Sheila Ngọc Phạm, 'Western Sydney is dead, long live Western Sydney!'

In the quiet, hilly suburb of Yagoona, from up on the rise of Graf Park, where the Cooks River begins in a rocky little scoop in the corner, roofs glint through the trees and a young woman in a hijab walks laps around the oval while talking on her phone. Along the streets, flags of different countries drape from houses and poles in the yards of Federation cottages and fibros. Between these older, more organic-seeming houses spring sharp-bricked duplexes, a sign of Sydney's latest push towards higher density. This area, like much of the south-west, has seen waves of immigration over the years – it was once known as Irishtown and also housed ten-pound Poms and post–World War II migrants from Europe. Since the migration of Lebanese and Vietnamese from the late 1970s and 1980s, this area has been particularly enriched by the cultural lives of these diasporic communities.

The writing and personal history of local resident Sheila Ngọc Phạm emit the sense that though in Sydney we may be far from other lands, we live out our days amid the flows of the world's currents. In walks of the suburban streets, in interactions with family and community – buying food, taking the kids to dance classes, spending time at the local library – we crisscross time and place and sow the seeds of the future in every exchange.

Sheila's autobiographical essay 'An Elite Education' recalls the day that her partner Josh and then prime minister John Howard were awarded degrees at her alma mater, the University of Sydney. The essay is illustrated, captivatingly, by a blurry photograph of Sheila, fresh-faced and beaming, with a grinning Howard, arm around her. The image forms an unreliable surface through which she delves into class, education and migration via Howard's exclusionary rhetoric, Sheila and Josh's education in this 'elite' institution, and their family's political and cultural histories. The picture is actually from an earlier encounter with Howard, during the Sydney Olympics in 2000, where teenage Sheila had worked poolside as a runner for the American broadcaster NBC. Spotting Howard, she asked for a snap, and he asked her: 'So where are you from?' Sheila holds this question, from such a speaker, up to the light, exploring its assumptions and contexts. This is her way: to probe questions of belonging with a critical curiosity, taking the reader with her into pathways of illumination and discovery.

Many such questions for Sheila are located in place and her upbringing amid refugee diasporas in the south-west of Sydney. A walk with her, from residential Yagoona into the heart of Vietnamese Bankstown follows threads of neighbourly connection, community art-making and activism, food culture and family. Fittingly, given the lively currents running through this part of Sydney, the name Yagoona means *today*, or *now*, in the Sydney district Aboriginal language, as recorded by the colonists of the First Fleet.

The walk begins at Sheila's house on a generous block. A wall of the living room is lined with books, and life is unfolding amid the flows of activity of a person with small children, a job, a writing career and a PhD underway. Heading out along the front path to the quiet sunny street, Sheila says that they have real estate agents knocking on their door on a regular basis, looking for properties to turn over to buyers eager to knock down and build duplexes. All up and down these streets are mid-twentieth-century houses on a modest scale with the sort of yard in which you can grow vegies, play cricket, or build a big shed for your work or projects: the kind of space that is very attractive to young families.

Sheila returned to the area more than six years ago after living in other parts of Sydney and the world, having grown up in the bushier Georges Hall, a few suburbs west, her family home a stone's throw from where Prospect Creek flows into the Georges River. It's been an adjustment for her to settle down with children after a relatively free-ranging decade from her mid-twenties to mid-thirties. But it was pandemic walks with her small children that drew her more deeply into the local community. Walking with her children to a local daycare centre, Sheila would start to recognise plants and food in certain gardens. She points out a pretty house, pale yellow against the blue sky, a silvery olive tree at the front, opening up a portal to the Mediterranean. 'We would admire this olive tree, and started talking to the Druze Lebanese owner, who runs a salon from his garage. Now we all come here for haircuts from him. Recently we went apple picking in the Blue Mountains and dropped off a bag. He's become a grandfather-like figure to my kids.' There's another house nearby with an overhanging basil bush, where you might nip off a handful. Kumquats and lemons hang over the street, temptingly.

On the way to the busy Hume Highway is the medical practice that looked after Sheila through her second pregnancy and the raising of small children. She appreciates the fact that she can access so many services locally, and yet on the block before the highway there's a row of closed businesses – hit, at least in part, by the periods of lockdown. In an article about the pressures on Western Sydney businesses and workers during Covid, Sheila writes:

> Ali, who runs the local Lebanese bakery, no longer has construction workers and schoolkids stopping by. Duc and Tina, who run a popular cafe in Bankstown, made the hard decision to close indefinitely. They live in the Fairfield LGA and crossing the border at the 'Meccano Set' arrangement of traffic lights on the Hume Highway every day would have meant being tested every three days for uncertain financial gain.

She writes of her work in public health ethics, how interventions are driven by utilitarianism: the greatest good for the greatest number. But there's a moral cost, the suffering of a minority, and during Covid, in Sydney, this is where it was felt, the community heavily policed while simultaneously relied upon by the rest of the city for its service workers.

At the busy intersection of Rookwood Road and the Hume Highway, a shuttered newsagency and a former video store sit forlornly on a corner engulfed by the Three Swallows Hotel. Across the highway, Chapel Road runs down the hill towards Bankstown and it's a different environment again, after the quiet streets of Yagoona and the roaring trucks of the highway; this is a pleasant semi-urban street of schools, churches and the TAFE, smart townhouses, medium-sized apartment blocks, large gum trees along the footpath. Passing St Felix, a Catholic primary school with a good reputation, Sheila says that she's committed to public schools. 'But religion is a constant conversation with my kids, especially my daughter. All her friends are Muslim. She goes to a public school in Bankstown. She asks questions about our religion and cultural practices – just trying to work out where she fits in with everything.' Her daughter is involved in Irish dancing, an activity new to Sheila's own Vietnamese family and her partner's mostly English and Scottish background. 'We care about questions of culture and language and identity – I'm trying to raise my kids in a very multicultural way.'

Close to the civic square of Bankstown, there's a church, St Paul's Anglican, the site of a familiar Sydney battle between preservation and development. The rector is fighting the congregation's proposed heritage protections because he says that without investment and development the building will decay, while local historians wish to protect the architectural features of the church and the memories enshrined there: soldiers' memorials, a priest's ashes interred beneath the altar. There is a fear too of an out-of-proportion tower block, changing the character of this medium-density streetscape. 'The thing about living here is the tension between the old and the new. What's worth preserving? What do we keep from the past? What do we replace it with?'

Sheila was at the recent council meeting where the church's

fate happened to be under discussion, attending as a member of the Climate Action Network for Canterbury Bankstown. 'We want to push Council to plant more trees; there's not enough coverage. You look around, and one big difference between here and say, Gordon, is trees.' In spite of beautiful parks, private gardens and bush areas, the streets of many areas in the west don't have adequate tree cover for a heating climate. A tree-cover map of Sydney shows, as Sheila suggests, that the north-eastern section of Sydney has much higher cover than the west, although it is improving. The climate in the west of Sydney is more extreme than on the coast and so the need for good air and shade is doubly important to keep life pleasant and walks possible.

This street down to Bankstown is a main walking route in Sheila's life, leading to many of the services and activities of family, work and artistic life. Looming at the end of it is the new Western Sydney University stack of sunset-coloured blocks. 'It shows, symbolically, how much the role of the university has changed. It has the shiniest, biggest office block in the entire city.' Also up ahead is the new library, opposite the old library of Sheila's childhood. 'The day I finished my HSC – it was a chemistry exam – I had an interview lined up at Bankstown Library. There are a lot of markers of my childhood that still exist here.' Her parents still live in the same house in Georges Hall, and her movements through these suburbs overlay old familiar routes.

Approaching the new library, Sheila reflects on growing up in the area. She speculates that the 'Anglos' she grew up with left for areas like Epping and Ryde in the north-west, or Menai and the Sutherland Shire in the south. There's a 'pull people feel towards being amongst their own kind – not just for white people. Some groups, Vietnamese or Lebanese, feel this community is more attractive.' These decisions are often shaped by class; there are newer, more transnational migrants who wouldn't choose this area: 'It seems like a bit of a ghetto to them. They don't understand these areas. There's no history for them.' Sheila references commentary by the journalist George Megalogenis about the different attachment patterns of migrants in Australia. For post–World War II migrants like Megalogenis's Greek parents and Sheila's refugee parents, 'the children of those migrants are much more invested in the idea of being Australian and contributing than migrants who could live anywhere. My parents, for example, left Vietnam in 1980, and up till now they've never gone back.' Sheila made her own emotional first visit when she was twenty-nine but, as for so many Australians, 'There's a huge gulf in my life about the old country.'

Sheila examines the complexities of diasporic belonging in a piece titled 'Flags of My Father', considering how time and generational distance bring different understandings of home and its symbols. As she writes, 'the older generations of Vietnamese-Australians have now lived more years in Australia than they lived in Vietnam, and the younger generations have grown up far away from the old country'. On her father's lawn there is an Australian flag faded by the strong sun, hanging proudly from a handmade flagpole. A significant presence in her childhood too was the South Vietnamese flag, no longer the official flag of Vietnam but a symbol of great cultural significance and emotion. As a child she would hear the old anthem of pre-communist Vietnam within her community: 'I didn't understand the formal language being sung because of my limited Vietnamese vocabulary, but I could feel myself choking up all the same.' While Sheila's dad forms a strong attachment to the Australian flag, Sheila comes to mistrust it, knowing it was wrapped around the bodies of young white men during the Cronulla riots in nationalistic display.

On the broad plaza at Paul Keating Park, the Bryan Brown Theatre is in keeping with the old library across the square, mid-century concrete with pointed column windows. In the foyer of the theatre, Bryan Brown's face looms cheekily from large banners. He's a famous figure from the area, growing up in Panania and coming to Bankstown to swim and watch movies. Sheila mentions the clip of him at the National Press Club in which he says, 'My name is Bryan Brown, and I'm a westie.' He's a patron of various organisations in Western Sydney and that note of defiance says something about the area's historical underdog status.

You can walk straight through from the theatre to the airy new library that opened in 2014, where Sheila spent time writing her PhD. As a young woman, when Sheila was a student at the University of Sydney, she would come home to a shift or two a week at the old Bankstown Library, shelving books. From her studious childhood into adulthood, 'the library always felt like a second home'. She wrote in defence of public libraries in response to a notorious piece in *The Washington Post* which asserted that libraries were no longer an effective use of public money in the age of Amazon. These spaces, of course, do much more than lend you books. They provided Sheila with refuge as a lonely child, and when she came to work in one, she observed people without homes making a space for themselves in these welcoming institutions. Now in the libraries in which she spends her time, she writes, 'there's a great deal of cultural diversity ... white men, women in hijabs, Chinese grandparents – all within metres of each other, sharing the same space'.

Along the mall is the Hoyts complex and the expansive carparks of Bankstown Central shopping centre, known forever to locals as Bankstown Square, where Sheila once worked in a music store. 'This was a major landmark of my childhood. I've been coming to the shopping centre for more than thirty years.' Hoyts was another major hangout. This common suburban childhood, lived between school and the mall and the movie theatre and the library, means that a 'narrative of deficit and deprivation' of Western Sydney doesn't make sense for Sheila. What she felt she was missing was something else: travel. One thought was: 'I'd love to go to America.' All around are the contemporary textures of the suburban mall – subtle lighting, mock timber – where today's teenagers live out their own restless urges. 'I thought growing up in Australia was a boring, daggy place ... when I was growing up I got to see movies, I got to go to the shops, I didn't necessarily think that I was worse off than anyone else.' Another experience of later childhood was the arrival of the internet, as she was growing up and 'yearning for the outside world'. With friends, in the school library, she would chat to people in America. 'We found it thrilling. I felt connected to other places and people. Technology has been a great enabler in my life.'

It's busy in the food court; there are lots of Muslim women eating lunch together, laughing, looking after children. The scene of women hanging out for a weekday lunch is enviable: 'they're very socially connected'. It's much livelier than many suburban shopping centres in Sydney, which can be bleak places, unchanged since the 1980s, or the overwhelming, bright Westfields with their airport-like stretches of glitzy consumerism. There's a broad square where you can buy groceries, passing between the spice shop, greengrocer and Lina's Deli. The displays of tins and treats and fresh food at the counter draw you inside, promising treasures like a shop in a vividly illustrated children's book. It is a favourite of Sheila's –

Lina's was always here in some form. 'I remember, as a kid, we would walk past it but never go in. My parents didn't shop there. Being Vietnamese, they didn't know this kind of food. But I would look at it longingly. And there's a smell. I can smell it now, a particular smell that delis have.' It reminds her of her time in Italy and Croatia – the Mediterranean released in the aroma of olives and cured meats. 'It brings me back to the idea of travelling the world, just being in Bankstown.'

Sections of the mall have resisted the urge towards conformity. There are generic stretches of fashion chains but also Asian grocery stores and lively cafes. Sheila points out the clothes store Urban Culture, which sells modest fashion for Muslim women – soft, flowing dresses and pants in subtle colours, hijabs and scarves. 'When I come here I think about the past constantly, because of the continuity of experience. I have a lot of associations.' Going to school locally, she knew Lebanese girls from the classroom. 'Something we had in common was that our parents were strict – I wasn't going on school camps either.' The sense is clear of a person with long memories of a place, continually navigating the streams of memory at the same time as walking her children to their activities, or choosing treats at the deli: memories that take her not just into the past but into the larger world that has shaped this community.

Emerging from the labyrinth of the mall, cutting through the station, you come to South Terrace. The strip has the in-between feeling of many such sites in Sydney, with the rail line being converted to the new Metro. Pigeons and ibis loiter among the people moving between the trains, buses and shops. This street has an appealing upper level, above the shops, an evocative line of 1920s and '30s shop tops wending down the hill in either direction. Sheila notes the work of Mylyn Nguyen, who has reproduced some of these buildings as exquisite paper miniatures. You can see these treasures online on Instagram, where Mylyn stands in front of a Bankstown building holding its tiny replica in her hand, or posts a clip of how to fashion a dog smaller than her fingernail.

Down the hill from the station to the right is Saigon Place, a section of Chapel Road that has its own tangible atmosphere, a zingy blend of Sydney and South-East Asia. A wonderful bustle fills the street lined with greengrocers, butchers, fish shops, restaurants, shops filled with cooking implements. There's the sound of people quietly talking, a small, old-fashioned-looking plane flying overhead from the airport at Bankstown, spicy-sweet cooking smells. As your gaze travels up from shopfront level there are bright red Vietnamese signs over the doors, Art Deco façades, tree branches against a brilliant blue sky.

Sheila greets a couple of people within the space of a minute or so as we head down past the enormous greengrocer with its wide shopfront and wonderful displays of produce, including treats like custard apples and special condiments. Such abundance has been a bonus since she moved back here, this food bringing 'continuity of culture and connection. My mum still cooks for us sometimes.' She points out a restaurant she's been coming to for thirty-five years, where one of her family's boarders from her childhood used to work as a cook. Sheila loves the street life here, reminiscent of elsewhere. 'You go to Vietnam, you go to Lebanon or many parts of the world – there aren't the seemingly empty neighbourhoods you see in some parts of Sydney.'

At the bottom of Saigon Place, where three streets meet – Olympic Parade, Greenfield Parade and Chapel Road – is a large sculpture of a bronze drum, a replica of one of Vietnam's 'National Treasures', the Ngọc Lũ Drum, an artefact of the

Bronze Age civilisation in the Red River Delta. It's an imposing object, satisfying in its roundness, large and ancient looking amid the flow of everyday life. Sheila talks of the work of Victoria Pham and James Nguyen, who have been working with such Đông Sơn drums to create new ways of making music and connecting to a culture's past. A profile of their work explores the project; for the artists, 'the drum sparked connections to their families, Vietnamese culture and mythology, and other artists. Both recall hearing stories about the ancient drums from their parents.' Sheila has collaborated with them, as well as including them in an exhibition she curated at the Fairfield City Museum & Gallery. 'We're trying to rematriate the drum and make it live again as part of contemporary culture, for us to reclaim some of that heritage. This drum is very meaningful for the Vietnamese.'

A couple of quick right turns from the drum is the Bankstown Arts Centre, a significant location for Sheila both in terms of producing cultural events and bringing her children to art and dance classes. Outside there's an installation among the trees – *Rolling Musical Screech* by Sue Pedley – that depicts Australian birds with signs describing their call: 'shrill brassy piping *wirra wirra wirra* far-carrying *kooeel*'. Passing into the garden courtyard of the arts centre, Sheila explains what's happening here: the work of the youth arts organisation Outloud, artists' exhibitions, events for Writing NSW and Utp (previously Urban Theatre Projects), and the Bankstown Poetry Slam – a lively, heartfelt event in which local writers tell their stories amid laughter and cheers. 'Council spending on the arts is so low – the centre really punches above its weight.' Sheila stops for a chat with one of the staff, saying she'll be back with her daughter later for a class.

On the site of the Arts Centre once sat Bankstown

Baths, one of Sydney's first Olympic-sized swimming pools and, as Sheila notes, a different kind of community space. Writing about the baths, Bryan Brown recalls a childhood of freedom and adventure – and the smell of the chlorine – for the kids from the public housing in surrounding suburbs. Like Sheila, he appreciates that one kind of community space has transformed into another: sitting at Bankstown Poetry Slam, he realises where he is and is happy to be among 'this audience of Lebanese, Egyptian, Chinese, Pakistani, Indian and Anglo Australians', a community hub for all ages.

There are plans to further rejuvenate this quiet fringe of Bankstown; Griffith Park on the other side of Olympic Parade has recently been the focus of an architectural competition. The concept pictures show a pergola with a sculpted ceiling curving around attractive native grasses and rocky play areas. On the side wall of the florist opposite are painted huge flowers, one of many colourful murals around Bankstown. The artist, Christina Huynh, has made several local artworks and appeared in Sheila's exhibition at the Fairfield Gallery. 'I love street art,' Sheila says. 'I really appreciate these pictures.' Christina's flowers are part of Sheila's toing and froing around the neighbourhood and down to the Arts Centre and so have become one of the texture of her days.

Wandering back into the Vietnamese area of Bankstown, we reach a narrow arcade that houses Sheila's favourite patisserie. Here she has ordered her kids' birthday cakes and, on one occasion, hundreds of mooncakes for the Moon Festival at Bankstown Arts Centre. 'I love having those kind of local relationships – that's what community is: relying on people. It's a stress of modern life and parenting that people just do too much themselves all the time.' She describes the bakery style as 'Vietnamese old school, French influence' with flavours like cassava. 'It's the same kind of taste for my children that I had – I like that continuity.' She points out her favourite restaurant – all of these places, tucked in arcades or off the street, conjure another world, far from Sydney, the sort of little hole in the wall where if you don't have the language you point at something interesting and an unbelievable meal arrives on your table in two minutes flat. This morning, Sheila has a piece for Monocle Radio's *The Menu* being broadcast from London; it's about eating in Cabramatta, another neighbourhood of southwest Sydney with Vietnamese and other South-East Asian and Chinese food influences. It bothered her that only Leichhardt and Carriageworks had featured in Monocle Radio's reports on Sydney food neighbourhoods, so she made them a food travelogue of Cabramatta, offering mouth-watering details of another area of Sydney vivified by migrant culture.

This part of Bankstown is dominated by the Bankstown Sports Club – 'it just gets bigger and bigger'. It's another venue Sheila visits for her daughter's dancing – there was an international meet-up for Irish dancing there recently. It's also a place that has been part of her writing life in Bankstown; she recalls visiting one time with a group of writers after a Sydney Writers' Festival event held at the Bankstown Arts Centre. There's a fake rainforest inside, and an Italian piazza – also, a train station–themed restaurant. There are incongruities for her in the ways different areas of her life take shape in this place. 'It's odd for me to think this has been part of my literary life.' The venues might sometimes be surprising, but 'living here inspires my own thinking about life and community – it informs my writing practice in a lot of ways – not just this area but Cabramatta and the surrounding areas as well.'

Back on Greenfield Parade, we pass a restaurant – An – with a queue out the door, famous for its phở, drawing visitors from across Sydney. It is impossible to go for a walk around Bankstown and not find yourself lured into one of its places to eat, and so lunch is calling, at one of Bankstown's humble but inviting cafes, Kinx, opposite the library back up Chapel Road. On the way there, through a laneway connecting Marion Street and Kitchener Parade, are more striking murals, these by the artist Thomas Jackson, of native Australian birds – two spotted pardalotes, an eastern koel and an azure kingfisher, large and vibrant on the side of a lawyer's office.

As the walk draws to a close, Sheila quotes a phrase she values and often dwells upon from the work of Vanessa Berry about taking in the details of the Sydney suburbs: the 'radical potential of taking notice'. These artworks, the murals enlivening the sides of unremarkable buildings, the lovely miniatures of Mylyn Nguyen, the replica gong and other details Sheila has noted on this walk, remind her of this – to look up, to remember, to consider what the details of place mean, to explore further histories and connections. The past is immediate and these prompts and portals open up new worlds every day. 'I can't just talk about something that's happened right this moment – that's just the surface. All we need to do is peel back one or two years, and then five years, ten, fifty – and there's all this other history beneath.'

TIDAL CITY

RUSHCUTTERS BAY PARK
AND ELIZABETH BAY

WITH
DELIA FALCONER

Like Los Angeles, with which it is sometimes unfavourably compared, Sydney's misty sunshine is never far from noir. And like Los Angeles, an Art Deco golden age cast its features – its Bridge, its Luna Park, its mission-style mansions like 'Boomerang', its palms – into a smile ... But to Deco lightness, in Sydney's case, you have to add sandstone as a kind of base note, an ever-present reminder of its Georgian beginnings and more ancient past. To that mix again, you have to add water, which penetrates the city with bright fingers, filters constantly through its foundations, and weighs down the air.

– Delia Falconer, *Sydney*

Curved around the parks of Rushcutters Bay and Elizabeth Bay, higgledy-piggledy apartment buildings climb the sandstone ridges, windows angled towards the harbour. The north shore opposite, its grey-green bush hovering above the water, can be glimpsed through yacht masts and the ferries chugging by to Watsons Bay and Manly. This area is expensive now, but in the 1920s, an enduring Australian bohemia was fashioned by writers and artists as they took up residence in the Art Deco apartment blocks and nineteenth-century mansions honeycombed with cheap bedsits. Here the city's dreamers made a new kind of life between the shifting delights of the land's edge and the urban pleasures of the Cross.

Novelist and essayist Delia Falconer is the author of *Sydney*, a personal and cultural history of the city, in which this area features prominently. She takes as her epigraph a section of the poem 'Five Bells' by the most famous of local bohemian poets,

Kenneth Slessor. Speaking on ABC Radio National, Delia attributed the poem's enduring popularity to its expression of the 'turbulent deep time moving around in the harbour'. Delia's own writing too is attuned to the way time works on Sydney's materials, as read in sandstone, trees, the shape of the land and movement of water.

The walk begins on the eastern side of Rushcutters Bay Park, below the ritzy suburb of Darling Point. Delia lived on the border of Rushcutters Bay and Elizabeth Bay for many years and this is the circuit she made most days, and still enjoys, visiting familiar landmarks, trees and creatures, 'going around the neighbourhood checking to see if everyone's home'. On the footpath close to New Beach Road is a stand of plane trees, their trunks mottled grey, their hollows home to many creatures: cockatoos, lorikeets, microbats. 'The old-growth native trees with their nesting hollows are becoming scarcer in the bush,' Delia says, 'but in this affluent urban space the creatures are making do and finding their own homes.' Along the perimeter of the park is a shadowy grove of figs with a mysterious grotto-like atmosphere. 'They have these roots and limbs that I always find magical to look at because they're so scarred and roped – almost like bodies. At dusk in summer I'd expect to see a dozen or so big, heavy flying foxes squabbling and eating the fruit, and that means that beneath the Moreton Bay figs you will be walking on this funky, dense layer of Milo-like crushed seeds and dried pulp.' As the path reaches the seawall there's a stand of flaky paperbarks, their trunks hanging with what looks like decomposing print or ancient layers of skin. 'I love the shagginess of this area. There's been a seismic shift socioeconomically, and yet there's something irrepressible and hard to contain about the geography itself.'

A forest of yacht masts crowds the bay; you could almost

run across the water from deck to deck. On the eastern shore is the Cruising Yacht Club of Australia, host to the Sydney to Hobart Yacht Race on Boxing Day each year. 'It's very busy in the week or two leading up to the race, everyone getting the maxi yachts into shape.' The presence of the yachts bestows a more frequent gift when the afternoon breeze arrives: 'that fantastic clinking of the rigging against the masts, a Sydney equivalent of the Florence church bells'. Lovely too is the curved seawall, made of sandstone blocks in the Victorian era, encrusted with lichens and sea creatures so that it has become a feature of the landscape both crafted and organic. 'The sandstone turns a mauve hue when the light turns blue in the evening. It's a beautiful, beautiful colour.'

Like the perfect curve of the bay, the topography of this park, flat and green, is artificial. Formerly sandhills and swamp – the rush-cutters of the early colony gathered the grasses for thatch – it was flattened and reclaimed in the late nineteenth century. 'You have this long, defined curve of the sandstone and yet the actual geography here would have been quite craggy and dynamic. Denis Byrne, a geographer, talks about Sydney as a city of spectral beaches and mudflats that have been pressed down under the landfill, made up of sand extracted from the old sandhills and bits and pieces of rubbish. Underneath that you have the coastal swamp geography still preserved. That's one of the reasons, I think, why these old inner suburbs can feel eerie, because the lay of the land is not the lay of the land at settlement.'

At the same time the layers of sandstone beneath the park, and the great slabs of it into which the city's harbour suburbs are cut, give the place a distinctive feel. 'Whenever I'm here I feel happy. We're on sandstone country – below our feet are six kilometres of it. If you walk up on the ridge along Darling Point

Road, you have that sense that as soon as any rain lands, the ground quickly dries out. It's not great for gardens; the water filters down into the sandstone and comes out through the cliffs. The suburb has a particular sort of smell: there's always a sense of dryness I really like, beneath the humidity and the umami harbour scents, that is almost particulate and makes me think of walking in the Blue Mountains.' Talking about sandstone on ABC Radio National, Delia spoke of vivid childhood memories, walking with her parents in the city where the roads were cut through the cliffs in The Rocks. She had 'this sense of the sandstone being very alive, almost a friendly kind of stone, because there used to be these great big sandstone walls, weeping, days after rain'.

The city, with its grand colonial buildings and barnacle-encrusted seawalls, has been shaped of this material, which formed this country long before it was quarried for bricks. 'We're standing above the fossilised floodplain of a Triassic-era river the size of the Ganges, which flowed from Antarctica when this area was far inland, and laid down all the sandstone. The harbour valley itself was carved out by the Parramatta River over many millions of years, then filled after the last ice age. The thing about sandstone is that a little crack will form in a seam – it's so porous – and over time it becomes incredibly carved, a beautiful and very sensuous geography.' The shaping of the conditions through the shifting forms of sandstone, water and weather are ever-present here on the edge of the harbour in this city characterised by flux. 'In Melbourne, the city's dominant stone is bluestone, which is a forbidding, adamant kind of stone. But many of Sydney's public buildings were built from this tabby-coloured sandstone, as Ruth Park described it, weathering before your eyes – so soft, so porous to lichen and pollution. And of course the unhewn sandstone is also so present.

It contributes to this being a very eventful landscape.' Delia mentions Helen Garner's essay 'Water Notes', written when Garner was living by Sydney Harbour. What Garner does, Delia says, 'is just, in fine detail, describe the shifts in the mood of the water and this act of paying attention – of ekphrasis – transforms into a story of acclimatising to the moods of the city, to its drama'.

At the western edge of Rushcutters Bay, foliage bursts out from between the apartment buildings on the artificially straight line of the foreshore. 'There were old colonial and nineteenth-century estates here, and you can see, looking out to the western edge of the bay, beyond where the seawall ends, how when they were broken up to build apartments, people thought, "I want more land." And so they put private walls in at the low point of the tide to extend their footprint. And then you have the bigger reclamation projects like this park, which were undertaken around the harbour from the early nineteenth century. "Reclaiming" land is an exercise in imagining the territory in a particular way, then putting a line in and filling it in to match that mental map, as if the outcome is inevitable. It's such a colonial term: reclaimed by who? It suggests that even land under water was destined to be "ours", to be wrested "back" from nature. But this area where we're standing would have been very likely busy and alive with human knowledge for thousands of years before the seawalls went in.'

Twenty thousand years ago, as Grace Karskens writes in *The Colony*, the harbour was a wide river valley heading out to the coast, up to twenty kilometres further east than currently. When the ice melted, the sea rose two metres a year. 'As some of the stories told by Aboriginal people today still relate,' she writes, 'country and campsites were lost as sea invaded land.' From the now sunken plains, sand blew in the southerlies to form the dunes of the eastern suburbs. Two thousand years ago, the water rose to one and a half metres higher than now, before falling back to current levels. Ian Hoskins, in his history of the harbour, imagines the replacement in the river valley of birds by fish: 'Only 8500 years ago, the water was fifteen metres below its present level. When the sea rise stopped some 2500 years later, schools of tailor and jewfish could swim where parrots and cuckoos may once have flown.'

'The Eora people,' Delia says, 'would have had their paths across this river valley and known it as Country that extended kilometres from the current coastline before it began to be slowly inundated by rising seas – and they would have seen the harbour stabilise at its current level. The seawall suggests solidity but I've always felt, since I was a child, and used to play in these reclaimed harbourside parks, that there's something unsettled about these weirdly flat, filled-in stretches. That they're places where something weird or unpredictable might happen. You're at this dynamic edge; there's the sense of Sydney and especially the eastern suburbs of Sydney of being on the edge of different ongoing layers and of deep time.'

The path along the curve of the sandstone wall leads to the park's spine, Rushcutters Creek – now a concrete-lined canal that channels the water's tidal flow inland, beneath busy New South Head Road, towards Edgecliff. Here Delia once saw a large stingray, a metre across, heading up the paved channel towards the eastern suburbs. The creek, one of several that fed into the swamp catchment, once ran downhill from present-day Oxford Street, near the back of today's St Vincent's Hospital. A large river red gum near the Reg Bartley Oval is the only reminder of the old Barcom Glen bushland that once ran along its sloping Darlinghurst side, the site of one of several Aboriginal settlements around Rushcutters Bay and in use until at least the 1860s. It gave the people access to water and was close to the fishing grounds in the mudflats now buried beneath the park. The edges of the canal articulate the layers of life here, the ways that time and settlement work on the landscape. Oysters cling to the bottom of the Victorian sandstone blocks of the wall, some of which are patterned in various holey and flaky layers, 'like lacework or pastry'. One side of the creek is planted with figs and mangroves, leaves dipping to the water. The flow of the water is controlled, the creek lined with concrete, but 'this is quite a dynamic tidal creek, so it's still remembering its old path'. The king tides erode the sandstone, surging over these edges. 'They say that the divisions between the postcodes of Sydney are often based on the old creeks and streams, and people along the creek's old course near Paddington's Boundary Street find that their houses still experience those flows of water when it wells up into their properties after heavy rain.'

Delia notes that in the 1940s Bea Miles, the Shakespeare-quoting rebel eccentric of bohemian Sydney, lived in a cave, no longer in existence, down here by the stormwater canal, with other homeless people. Now there is a fence. Kate Grenville's fictional version of Bea, in her book *Lilian's Story*, is Lil, who lives in the park, unwrapping herself from a bundle of newspapers in the morning: 'I heard the city wake slowly, and the birds take second place as hurrying men in suits and women in high heels began to clatter along the paths to the city, and everyone got ready to die another day away.'

Past Reg Bartley Oval, up the hill of Waratah Street towards Elizabeth Bay, literary sites begin to gather. Beyond the junction with Roslyn Gardens, to the left, is a large aged care facility, St Luke's, which has all but swallowed Lulworth House, Patrick White's childhood home and the model for houses in *Voss* and *The Vivisector*. 'The lower side of the street where the apartments are would have been rocky bushland – White writes about going down through the wild bush from the house down to the water.' The terrain is still rugged, in spite of the streets of villas and units. All along Roslyn Gardens, slabs of sandstone cliff face, possibly part of one of the area's many quarries, are visible between the apartment buildings and carparks. Through the bars of a fence, the layers of Sydney's past can be seen in the dramatically craggy cliff, the sandstone bricks along its top, above them the windows and trim white lines of a modern apartment block up on Elizabeth Bay Road. Figs grow from the wall, roots trailing, and other plants – 'opportunists' – spread from the fissures in the sandstone. 'In Sydney, the land tilts up so that the cliffs rear above the sea, which is unusual. There was a seismic event where the sandstone basin was pushed up and to the water's edge. You can see that violence here as well as the gentle accretion of the layers of the huge riverbed.'

The layers of times past on a more recent scale continue with the mix of architectural styles along Roslyn Gardens as you climb towards Ithaca Road: The Wroxton, an Art Deco building with curved balconies and 'the most gorgeous timber-panelled lobby'; the hugely grand Brent Terraces, a row of Victorian homes – songwriter Don Walker lived in one, former prime minister Paul Keating in another – next to a wall from an old estate being reclaimed by little flowers. When Delia first came here in the early 2000s, there were fabulous old TV stars, one with a magnificent beehive and spangled jackets, a society photographer who matched his eye patch to his tennis whites or tuxedo, gentle Bob who sold *The Big Issue* at the markets in a tutu, publishing people, writers, painters. Delia's neighbour and friend, the writer and translator Linda Jaivin, wrote in 2005 of the rich sense of the bohemian character of these streets around Kings Cross, but a strong feeling too of the threat to a way of life – the gleaming high-rises replacing the 'old hotels that contributed so much to the character of the place', moneyed newcomers' resistance to what the actor Nell Schofield described as 'life in all its feral glory'.

On a street corner a fig spreads its own feral glory between and almost into the apartments. On closer inspection, it seems a cabbage palm is growing from between its branches, fig roots wrapped around the base of it as though they are locked in struggle. 'It's another of the area's beacons for flying foxes, "windrowing", as poet Les Murray puts it, across the suburb each dusk from their camp in Centennial Park to feed. By day, swifts wheel above the branches. Little City of Sydney carts come through to clean up the layers of decaying matter and seeds: it's Sisyphean work. The trees are like a metropolis in themselves.'

The thrilling mishmash of apartment buildings, placed at odd angles according to the topography, continues up towards the crest of the hill at Elizabeth Bay Road. A little to the east on the loop of Macleay Reserve is the Manhattan-esque 'Gotham City' (officially Adereham Hall), looming above all wanderings in these suburbs because of its height and location up on the ridge. It is also a site of suicides. Ithaca Gardens, a 1960s brick apartment block, is one of several mid-century Harry Seidler buildings in the area. Walking down Ithaca Road towards the harbour you catch a glimpse of the back of the Blackstone on Onslow Avenue, a handsome building from 1920 in the neoclassical tradition. 'When I pass the Blackstone,' Delia says, 'I always think of playwright and novelist Sumner Locke Elliott's autobiographical novel *Fairyland*, in which his hero begins to find love with other men in these local buildings in the 1930s and '40s. And I think of other memoirs of sexual liberation set later, during World War II; American sailors on R&R in Kings

Cross were spending the night in these apartments. This was bohemian heartland.'

Past the Deco blocks Ithaca and Winston, with their brass bells and gracefully designed glass doors, and the famed 1920s Spanish Mission–style Boomerang, lies the small green crescent of Beare Park and the glimmer of Elizabeth Bay. This pretty nook is another colonial land grab from the harbour. Before colonial times, local people fished on the beach here. Later, in the 1820s, the foreshore was the site of an experiment: the Macquaries' Elizabeth Town, an Aboriginal 'model village'. There was a row of bark huts, and the group was encouraged to grow crops. 'People used to come down in carriages to gawp.' The village didn't last – a massive land grant was awarded to colonial secretary Alexander Macleay in 1826 and he built Elizabeth Bay House above the bay, its remnant walls still running between buildings in the modern suburb.

Now this little park is a garden for the apartment dwellers, as well as a backpackers' and children's party venue, unofficial dog park and boot-camp gym. In its quieter moments, you might drink your coffee on a bench, ponder the massive cranes and masts of the Garden Island naval base, listen to the thump of a tinnie on the water. Lining the friendly yellow wall of a Mediterranean mansion are colourful kayaks, 'which accumulated guerilla-style during the Covid lockdowns'. A slick, architect-designed marina with a popular cafe has replaced a tin-shed jetty. From 2018 to 2019, as part of this revival, a little on-demand ferry – Sydney's first – briefly took commuters into the city. 'You'd putter out slowly past Garden Island, then they'd get towards the end and just floor it, dropping you at the Harbour Master Steps outside the Museum of Contemporary Art. It was one of the city's small delights that any person could experience with just an Opal card, an access to staggering beauty that I don't think you get would get so easily in other cities. When we first moved here, my partner used to keep a kayak here at the old marina for ten dollars a week and at night we would let ourselves in with the key to watch the moonlight on the flat water.'

A little way back up Ithaca Road is Billyard Avenue, where poet Kenneth Slessor lived in an apartment at 18A with a view of the naval warships, publishing 'Five Bells' just before the outbreak of war in 1939. Opposite Boomerang, at the end of a pathway between two apartment blocks, is a narrow cut-through and stairway up to Onslow Avenue above: 'It's public but you have to know it's there.' This damp nook between the apartment blocks is a secret place, a particularly intriguing remnant of Macleay's landscaped gardens. Delia describes it in a story, 'The Intimacy of the Table', in which a young poet remembers a night of drinking with Slessor:

> I seem to remember, although I have been unable to recognise the street again, that he took me through a breach in a wall behind a block of flats where there was a mossy grotto, its steps and niches carved into the cliff. It was all that remained of one of the colony's first gardens and the optimism of that time, he said.

An ornamental retaining wall of sandstone bricks incorporating a natural overhang with a carved date, 1835, opens up to a cave and a mossy decorative altar. There are marks of fire in the corners and, next to the folly, part of a sweeping stone staircase and convict-brick wall. 'Although there has been a lot of nineteenth-century interference with this particular site, I've often wondered, standing here, if it once sheltered Gadigal people, given the history of First Nations people using rock overhangs like these in the Sydney region as resting places and as places of refuge during the smallpox plague.' Another overhang-turned-grotto, further up Billyard Avenue, Delia says, was repurposed in the 1970s as a bus stop. On the way up the balustraded stairs towards Onslow Avenue, surviving between the flats, is a botanical remnant of Macleay's estate: a tall kauri pine from the formal gardens.

Emerging from the secret dark between the buildings, the bird sounds and traffic are suddenly louder. Macleay's mansion, Elizabeth Bay House, a little way north, still looks grandly out over the harbour. It is a stately building, part of the shift that, as Grace Karskens writes, took Sydney from being a 'crooked, intimate, compact' town to the 'rectilinear, polite and self-conscious city' of the Macquaries and Macleays. Even this grand building, though, was divided into bedsits in the 1940s and packed out with artists and writers.

In her essay 'A City of One's Own', Delia writes of the liberation the 'boom in apartment living on or near the harbour' from the 1920s offered to women in particular. 'These flats, some in new buildings and others bedsits carved out of once-grand homes, offered privacy, access to work and the intellectual life of the city, an escape from unpaid domestic labour and freedom from the watchful eyes of family and suburban neighbours.' In this essay she references the character Nora Porteous from Jessica Anderson's *Tirra Lirra by the River* who moves to Sydney with her overbearing husband in the late 1920s. She escapes daily from her marital apartment in the Potts Point mansion Crecy to another, Bomera, where she forms a close friendship with a gay man, watches artists frolicking in the pool and is taught the livelihood and art of dressmaking by her friend Ida. 'Once people would come to this neighbourhood,' Delia says, 'to live a less conventional sort of life. You were freed even from having to cook. These places wouldn't have originally had kitchens – they might have had a hotplate. You'd get your little bit of something that you would warm up from the corner shops. For many people who didn't fit in or were fleeing different types of trauma, it was a place of refuge. For women, the incredible liberation of not having to live under constant scrutiny was immense.'

The walk comes to an end on Elizabeth Bay Road, just around the corner from Kings Cross, the harbour glinting blue amid the steep labyrinth, bringing light and shimmer to the area's bohemian history. In *Sydney*, Delia connects the city's artistic temperament to its material textures: 'It is Sydney's wild mix of the stunning and unplanned, of glitz and rot … that gives it its very distinct cultural and intellectual life. In Sydney we are shaped spiritually by damp abrasion and the democracy of grit.'

'There's always a kind of turbulence, a moodiness,' Delia says now. 'We're a tidal city – you've got that constant change. The flux and moods of the harbour are an endless joy to me.'

WALKING ON CAMMERAYGAL COUNTRY

NORTH WILLOUGHBY AND MIDDLE COVE

WITH JAKELIN TROY

I am a member of the Ngyamitjimitung clan of the Ngarigu people of the Snowy Mountains, the alpine Country of New South Wales in southeastern Australia also known as the Monaro district ... I never left my Country, as we call our territories, and I was always a whole person in that snowy place. We are the 'ice mob,' people of a frozen landscape.

– Jakelin Troy, 'Standing on the Ground and Writing on the Sky'

Cammeraygal Country covers a large area of the Lower North Shore and beaches, a part of Sydney defined by craggy harbour shorelines, genteel suburban streets and spreading parks. These are coastal lands, the Country of the hunting and fishing Cammeraygal people. In the 1980s and 1990s, Professor Jakelin Troy, a Ngarigu woman of the Snowy Mountains region and anthropological linguistics scholar, collected what was known of the languages and dialects local to the Sydney area on the arrival of the First Fleet. Jaky, who lives between Canberra and an old family home in this part of Sydney, has studied indigenous languages, in Australia and further afield, for her entire career. Our walk on Cammeraygal Country, on which Jaky speaks of herself as a long-familiar, respectful visitor, encompasses the feeling too of her much colder, more mountainous Country, and of her work with other indigenous and mountain peoples.

The walk begins in the garden of Jaky's family home in North Willoughby, where all around the garden beds are large, smooth, pale rocks from the Snowy River, brought here by her grandfather so that her grandmother 'would always have a piece of the Snowy Mountains in her place in Sydney'. Jaky's grandfather worked on the Snowy Mountains Hydro-Electric Scheme, and carried these rocks home for his wife on the train. 'I'm surrounded by my Country. When I put my hands on these rocks, they're cold like the alpine waters.' Plants sprout between and over the rocks, embedding them in place.

This house is an old and familiar home to Jaky, belonging first to her grandparents and then her mother. 'The female line are all Aboriginal. All Ngarigu of the Snowy Mountains. My grandmother always had this great connection with other indigenous peoples, and peoples from marginalised and minority countries.' Her grandmother had friends from Pakistan before its partition from India, and her great-grandmother spent time in Fiji working with women there as a hospital matron, teaching them art practices from her home and good health practices in raising children. 'There's this line of women here who have engaged with other indigenous communities.' Jaky herself works with indigenous people in Pakistan and feels a strong link with other mountain people. 'Near Canberra, we have these soft, rolling mountains. They're high, but they're very eroded because Australia is such an ancient country, whereas in Northwest Pakistan, where I work, they have five of the fourteen highest mountains in the world. It's just peak after peak. They're known as the cloud mountain people.' Here in Australia, in her Country of the Snowies, the highest peak – officially Kosciuszko – is known as Kunama Namadgi. Jaky explains that Kunama means having the quality of snow, or 'snowy'; nama means breasts; –dgi denotes 'having'. 'Snowy boobies!'

Jaky has travelled to South America too, and feels a strong connection with the Andes. 'It's embodied in me. I like being cold, standing in the shade on a cold, cold morning.' It's fresh for Sydney today; in spite of the sunshine there's a chilly wind. 'I'm thriving at the moment. I love camping out in the cold and with frost. I used to do a lot of endurance horse riding. There was nothing I loved more than sleeping in a swag or in a little tent or in the horse float, the horses chomping in their yard nearby – and a campfire. It was cold and crisp and you'd get up really early in the morning. It was still dark and the brumbies all came out.'

Beyond the shelter of the pretty garden, filled with Jaky's grandmother's rocks and camellias, the driveway is a 'brush turkey place'. He's taken up residence and makes a familiar, hardworking neighbour. This 1920s California bungalow, with its generous land, neat pitched roof and long drive, was the 'urban dream for White Australia, which is funny because it's been occupied by Aboriginal people since the 1940s. So many generations have lived in this house.' There is long memory here, and continual connection to the mountains. 'Mountain people think about the sky being part of our Country as well, the stars. These ceilings were designed so that you look up and see something. It's got all these beautiful impressed patterns of flowers and fruits, and I've looked at it all my life because I've stayed here ever since I was a baby. It always evoked faraway places to me.'

Jaky's great-grandmother was born on Country in the high Snowies. As well as travelling the world, she and Jaky's grandmother moved constantly between the mountains and this warmer place, just as Jaky does for work, and as the people Jaky works with in Pakistan do. 'They travel up and down the valley. In the summer, they go up to the high pastures with their livestock and then, as the winter comes, they go back down the mountain to the flat country where it's warm for the rest of the year. That's how we as people were too and that's the lifestyle I live.' Her grandfather too commuted from here to Cooma after returning from the war, and Jaky's mother started a ski club in Thredbo where Jaky can stay and be on her mountain Country.

Out in the sun and wind on the broad street, Willoughby Park is a block or two's walk. It's a classic suburban Sydney park: a raised sports field, several stands of gums, a quite grand early twentieth-century building in the corner, a smart new playground amid the trees. Jaky went to preschool for a spell in the park and has known these trees as a child and as an adult. 'These trees are leopard gum. I've grown up with them. See the gymea lilies coming out? My mother told me, ever since I was little, that when the gymea lilies begin to flower the spring is coming.' The stately old eucalypts are wrapped in a beautifully patterned bark, mottled in muted greys. 'Look up the tree – you can see its turgid sap. It looks like a barley-sugar twist. These are a bit dangerous – it's the young limbs you've got to watch out for. These are things that I've been taught all my life.'

Wandering the avenue of gums, Jaky explains the way that First Nations people refer to trees. 'Because of the way Aboriginal languages work, you wouldn't name an entire tree. So for example, with the Gadi plant, the xanthorrhoea or grass tree: in the diagrams that were drawn of that by First Fleeters – the *Hunter Sketchbook* – John Hunter named the trunk, and then the bracts, with the leaves, and then the flower, the spike that has the flower on the end of it. And so all the different parts have different names. Overall it's the Gadi, but that's a European way of trying to taxonomise the whole plant.' To describe the plant as a whole in an Aboriginal language requires different terms according to its season, whether it's flowering, and so on. 'In Central Australia, there's a kangaroo bush – it's called that in high summer, when kangaroos rest under it. But at another time of the year it has another name.'

In European cultures, intricate plant knowledge is specialised: botanists, horticulturalists and keen gardeners are the ones who know the names of plants, and their forms and uses. 'In the Aboriginal language world everybody knows, because it's important knowledge that you need for every part of your life. What time of the year can you take the bark off the tree to use for making huts or canoes? What time of the year can you harvest fruits or flowers that you could soak in water and make a sweet drink? And what time of the year will certain animals be attracted that will be good to eat?'

One of the things that the local people just could not understand about the British was how unsophisticated they were in relationship to the environment. 'Why would you go and chop down a whole tree? There are reports of Aboriginal people trying to stop people chopping a tree down and hugging the tree and crying, because the tree is family – you know every tree.' As well, the British cut down important trees that had been used for ceremony. 'There's nothing in an Aboriginal environment that doesn't have a direct connection with you or a meaning for you. Every rock, every grain of sand: everything is animated.'

Jaky points out red sap oozing from silver bark that can be used as a kind of chewing gum. Even though she grew up on the coast, she is not as close to these Sydney trees, on someone else's Country, as she would be to those on her own. She has worked with local language and has known this park and these trees all her life, 'but they're not my Country people in the way that the snow gums are when I'm up in that Country, riding and walking and skiing. I live in Canberra, which is an extension of that alpine Country. I feel there that everything has a connection to me directly, whereas here I have a great respect, but I'm a visitor.' Standing here among these trees, appreciating their lives and gifts, is a form of acknowledgement, a way of engaging with this place.

One of the ways Jaky relates to Country, here and in the mountains, is to draw it, an autoethnographic process she describes in her essay 'Walking, Sketching and Dogs'. The 2019–20 fires on her Country and her feelings of loss led her to take walks, journalling, often creating a visual record of place in order to reflect on it. 'There's nothing I love better than drawing the bark of these trees. I love drawing all these gnarly textures.' She notes that the tree we are studying has kookaburras living in it. They've gone out for the day, but they'll be back at dusk. 'The chorus of kookaburras is just amazing as they're coming back to roost. For me, this is a natural place, a wildlife place, even though it's quite constructed. And the currawongs, they're different here from in my Country. When the currawongs come down from the mountains, they're grey currawongs, a lot of them. And you know it's going to snow. When they go back, the spring's coming.' Jaky retrieves from the ground a beautiful red leaf with just a touch of green so that she can draw it later. 'It's not just the act of drawing, it's like an act of loving that thing. It makes it part of me and my world.'

Heading away from the park, approaching Eastern Valley Way where traffic rushes by, it's concrete footpath underfoot: 'a more difficult space to be in' than amid the friendly ambience of old trees. Jaky greets a dog warmly; she has had many, as well as horses. In Canberra she rides around the suburbs and up the mountain. 'On a horse, nothing's really afraid of you – birds and animals, kangaroos. It's like having four legs instead of two and there's that relationship between that animal and myself. They're going along, having a look at things as well. I often take my sketchbook in my saddlebag and I'll sketch and paint while I'm riding. So I find that peripatetic practice by walking either on my own two legs or my four strong horsey legs, and going for long, long distances.'

Across the busy thoroughfare we follow Cawarrah Road into Middle Cove towards Middle Harbour and the traffic noise reduces to a distant hum. The terrain quickly shifts from the neat, wide streets of early twentieth-century bungalows and ordered gardens to the steep bushy headlands around the water. To the left of the street, houses are perched above on high slabs of sandstone; to the right, a wooden gate opens onto cool blue air. Gone are the lawns and trimmed hedges. Greenery gushes from the gaps in the sandstone, gums cram into the spaces between houses: lushness everywhere. 'Everything grows so quickly that I laugh at people trying to garden here. It's certainly colonised, but fundamentally, the bush has held its own. If we look down into this person's block here, there are big rock platforms. They may even have petroglyph carvings on them. They haven't modified it: the Country dictates how people live in it. If you look down there you can imagine rock pools, ceremonial places. And there's melaleuca – the paperbark. People use it for cooking. Women use it to make soft places for their babies. All over Australia, even in the most built-up areas of Sydney, you can still feel the Country and the people of the Country.'

The road becomes Highland Ridge, running along the spine of Middle Cove towards the bush of Harold Reid Reserve. Across the road is a pale gum that looks like a snow gum of the mountains: a large, strong tree. 'It's got these very twisty branches and when these trees get wet up in my Country you get this kind of lolly colouring – red and green and rust. And these scribbles are little beetles that get into the bark that are really important to the tree, but they get out of hand. Down in my Country now, there are all these trees that end up ringbarked by the larvae of this beetle. When the tree gets distressed by fire or not enough water, these things will take off.'

Cool air carries along this high road from the water. Jaky points out the bottlebrushes and grevilleas in the gardens that draw native bees with blue abdomens. Much about this place has remained itself in spite of the suburb that has grown up from it. 'The Country is constantly decolonising itself. It's the way I feel we are as Aboriginal people now. My own people are engaging with the practice of performing our snow song. My Elders and community who sing this song with me really love to sing it, and the more we sing our snow song, the colder it gets, and then it snows. I've been singing it lately in Sydney and it's really cold.' Jaky laughs and sings the song walking along the sunny street. She translates: 'Bring the snow, moon. Moon, bring the snow. We need the snow.' The snow is essential for the melt and the nourishment of the alpine bogs, for life's cycle to continue, and so it is an important ritual to sing it forth.

Beneath the feet now is a soft paperbark carpet amid sandstone escarpment and melaleuca and warm-red angophora. The view across the gully is of the bushy slopes of Castle Cove and beyond, the high ridge that runs down to the Northern Beaches in the east, where Jaky also spent much of her childhood. Below are the dreamy turquoise inlets and coves of Middle Harbour, roofs glinting amid the bush. The feeling of what this place was once, and is still, is very present. 'This is what it always was – you can see why the British wanted to keep this place, because it's just so glorious and easy to live in, once you figure out how to grow things. The Aboriginal community helped with that. Plenty of fish and things you could eat; they made sure people didn't poison themselves. Our way is to care for and incorporate people.' Jaky brings this practice back to language and naming. Bennelong, who was a 'very, very good languages man', and Governor Arthur Phillip gave each other kin names: biyana ('father') for Phillip, and duru ('son') for Bennelong. 'So there was this reciprocity always.'

All around these bumpy promontories are wonderful walking tracks. From here you can walk off the ridge down Harbour Lane to the Sugarloaf walking track in Harold Reid Reserve, a loop that takes you between curved sandstone walls out to the point, where a quiet cluster of landscape painters works to conjure the grey-green headlands and shining reaches of water. Further down towards the water, there's another, longer loop around the point. Here you are almost level with the dreamy mangroves, which appear to float out over the bays; above them on the far shore is the strange Innisfallen Castle, built in the early 1900s amid the bushland at Castle Cove, a weird anachronism.

In a book called *Everywhen*, which describes the Aboriginal cosmology of time, Jaky contributed an essay, 'Standing on the Ground and Writing on the Sky', about writing her history and using her language. In the essay she speaks of the emotions of recovering her language and song, of connecting with Country through arts practices and with the indigenous people of Pakistan through their shared grounding in high country. Walking back along the bushy ridge, Jaky describes the rewards and difficulties of this emotional approach to the past. 'I was trained in the good old days of anthropology where you have to be "etic" or "emic". This is stuck in my brain forever. You are either an insider or an outsider, and to do good-quality academic work you had to be objective – you had to position yourself outside. For me, emotional history is a way of truth telling, and it comes at a price, because first of all it means laying yourself bare and allowing people into your deepest thoughts and your sense of identity and community, and how you know who you are and what your place in the world is.' Her work has become about 'the emotional practice of letting myself feel: sharing how I feel about Country, sharing how I feel about my cultural practices. Singing, dancing, renewing the practice of Ngarigu language with my community.' She writes in the essay about how overwhelming it has been to speak this language in public: 'When I spoke my language for the first time, it was as if I were invoking my ancestors and at the same time mourning the loss of all that we were and all that we could have been.'

Crossing the busy road and onto the quiet suburban street past the park, Jaky explains that the experiences of our bodies as we walk are emotional too. 'We just walked down to look at that vista. That will stick with you. We're in this lovely, cool, sea environment – we're going between climates. This street is slightly higher, it's a bit warmer amongst all these trees. This is an emotional experience.' She speaks of her practice, making tiny artworks in her sketchbooks, using the earth and charcoal, 'engaging physically with the Country itself. Walking on Country, this is what we would have done as Aboriginal women – walked through Country – and we would have probably collected some things to take back and eat. There could be a bunch of kids following along behind us. What we've just done is, for me, culturally normal.'

Passing by the Anglican church opposite the park, Jaky remembers going to Sunday school here. Her family were socialists, and her mother said that Jesus was the first socialist revolutionary. 'My grandmother was farewelled here. She died in that house. All of this area has a spiritual meaning for me, but not as a Christian. We believe in the recycling of the spirit. My grandmother said to me in the garden when I was tiny, "When I'm gone, if you ever need to find me, just look and see those stars. They're all our ancestors and I will be up there. I'll be one of them and I'll be shining really brightly so you'll know it's me." She was just such a lovely person. And that's our belief system: that everyone comes back. A shooting star is someone coming back to be born again. Nothing ever ends.'

Back at the driveway that belongs to the brush turkey, Jaky talks of the Sydney language, which came to be known as Dharug, which she has worked to gather and record, and the renewal of it in recent decades. People used to talk about 'dead' languages but, in a way, the language has not even been sleeping. People had knowledge and have actively recovered more, and they have brought the language back into use. 'There was knowledge that community members had, they just weren't sharing.' It has been far from safe for Aboriginal people to use their languages and transmit them openly to their children. In this sense, language revival is part of the emotional history Jaky has been talking about, one that renews people's connection to Country while carrying the grief of their losses. 'The Dharug are here. The Gadigal, Cammeraygal, Wangal, the Gweagal down at La Perouse and all the people across Burramatta. Everybody in Sydney speaks their names, their clan names and their connection with Country. The Gadigal are responsible for the Gadi, the xanthorrhoea; the Burramattagal responsible for the eels, the Burra. This kind of responsibility: language is the way of articulating that. I love speaking Sydney language. Warami: hello. Everything you are is embodied in your language. Now people are renewing their languages. It's living, embodied and part of people's psyche, their cosmology, their engagement with place and with each other. It feels good to do it.'

How do you say thank you in Sydney language? 'Didjurigura. And when you say goodbye, you just say, "Yanu" – I'm off.'

Didjurigura, Jaky. Yanu.

SOME SECRET TO LIFE

CASULA AND LIVERPOOL

WITH MAX EASTON

Helen remembered that there were always rumours about that end of the Georges River being haunted by ghosts of poisoned factory workers and dead soldiers from the Holsworthy Barracks. She imagined that there would always be reports coming in of someone or something appearing somewhere near the walled fences of the apartments, because there really were movements in the night. About a half dozen locals squatted on the riverbanks in cheap tents and tarps under shrubbery and bridges. They lived peacefully in an array of self-managed lots, stable enough to run small veggie patches that got them by between runs into town. As the footprints of the revitalising high-rises crept closer to them, Helen imagined they would be beginning to lose their anonymity.

– Max Easton, *The Magpie Wing*

Driving along the ridge of the busy Hume Highway in Casula, stretches of grey-green bushland can be glimpsed beyond the townhouses and shopping strips. A few kilometres south of the towers of Liverpool's CBD, Casula Road tracks east into tidy suburban streets before plunging suddenly through tight curves and dense bush reserve to the station at the bottom of the hill. Green shade is all around, bellbirds chink. Novelist and music writer Max Easton grew up among the secret nooks of these suburbs around Liverpool in the south-west of Sydney, and his two novels *The Magpie Wing* and *Paradise Estate* follow the lives of its young people as they replace the tribalism of football with the punk and political scenes of inner-west share-houses. *The Magpie Wing* in particular captures these suburbs as the setting of restlessness and searching, of quests for connection and belonging on the footy fields, in the bedrooms and across the night-time parks of teenage Sydney.

This hidden corner, away from the eyes of adults, conjures moments of 'childhood mischief', and Casula Station, the starting point of this walk with Max, is the site in *The Magpie Wing* of early political rebellion. It's a quiet place, unstaffed, and in spite of its steel shelters and lifts it has the feel of a country station. In the time before ticket and Opal machines, the people of Casula were able to travel freely on the network. Seventeen-year-old Walt, stoked up by 'early forays into punk music, his granddad's radical history, and his printout of *The Anarchist's Cookbook*', reacts badly when a machine is finally installed, smuggling his amateur explosives down the hill in the dark to blow it up and doing just enough damage – melting the buttons, jamming the coin slot – to discourage further installations. Max created this scenario as 'an alternate reality. There was no ticket machine for a long time. Whenever they tried, it was vandalised – kicked in and smashed. I was always curious about who did that.'

Across the station bridge, two massive rusting water tanks, encircled with large letters, graffiti tags and art, create an atmosphere of ruin and urban re-use amid the trees and parkland. The Graffiti Tanks are part of Liverpool Power-house, a decommissioned mid-century electricity station, now an arts centre. 'These are *legal* graffiti walls,' the Powerhouse website explains, 'so register your name at reception beforehand to ensure you are covered if the police question you.' On the other side of the Powerhouse, children skate with penguin stabilisers on a pop-up ice rink. Beyond the buildings and a community garden, the Georges River flows between banks lined with wattle, gum and casuarina. The chiming of the bellbirds competes with the trains: the polite whoosh of the suburban service, the lengthy rumble of the goods train.

An inviting path leads towards Liverpool, running along between the river and rolling green parkland, previously a golf course. Max's first job as a teenager was at the golf course driving range at Tree Valley Golf Course in nearby Prestons, also being redeveloped, as a housing estate. 'I played golf occasionally with my dad. It was such a different culture at those clubs; it was a working-class activity. The price was low and the course was crap, poorly looked after – and there were the droughts as well. Because I worked there, I could play for free. My friends would come and hit the ball amongst the empty Woodstock cans. I didn't realise golf was more or less an elite sport until I was an adult.'

Along the path, a sign advises walkers encountering snakes to 'calmly walk the other way' while shiny towers up ahead – incongruous to someone who grew up here – announce the city centre of Liverpool. 'It feels like the science-fiction version of my childhood. There's some memory in the back of my mind that doesn't have the high-rises in the skyline – it's so strange and eerie to see them.' Long local knowledge includes the memory of what was there before. 'The thing with development in Sydney is that anything new has to strip something out. The old community and neighbourhood spots go when the new apartments come in – it's always really unsettled me.'

The M5 motorway bridge, flying over the parkland and river, marks the border between Casula and Liverpool, one of those suburbs of western Sydney, as Max writes, 'vilified and reduced to some kind of lawless subaltern non-state' by the media in the time of his childhood. But people have their own geographies, shaped by more personal forms of belonging: 'none of the ideas kicked around by faceless politicians and hack journalists really mattered. Because down the road at the Campbelltown Sports Ground, we had a team playing in the top rugby league competition in the world.' He says now, 'My understanding of Sydney geography as a kid was just rugby league teams. Western Suburbs played in Campbelltown, then there was Canterbury-Bankstown, there was Penrith and Parramatta. There were all these western Sydney clubs, and the train lines too: my idea of the distance between suburbs was the idealised train map, implanted in my head for so long.'

One of the memorable features in *The Magpie Wing* is a resistance to viewing central Sydney as a core in relation to a periphery. Like Max, his characters hop on trains and buses and in parents' and friends' cars and sometimes walk long distances to reach the other hubs in their networks: football clubs across the south-west, alternative record shops in Parramatta, suburban parks where kids are making mischief. For Max, his migrations might have been driven by 'a different cinema or a better Timezone'. The internet, coming just at the right time for a person born in the late 1980s, was another kind of expedition. As a teenager, Max was 'playing rugby league, trying to make that my thing, but there was also this itchiness, a feeling that there must be something else'. The internet opened up a portal to subcultures, scenes, special languages, identity. 'When we first got the internet in '97, our computer wasn't powerful enough to handle it, and then it was a long few years until Dad got round to upgrading. Once I started getting going in the early 2000s, all I wanted to do was find some secret to life.' He picked up the tangled threads of information, following his curiosity. 'I was interested in movies and professional wrestling but then you start grabbing onto different ideas. They'd come from the side: someone would insult someone on a message board and you're like, "What's *that* word?" and go looking for it. When you're a teenager you feel like a blank slate. The early internet felt so open. It really did feel like cyberspace to me.'

Above the river and park in the south-eastern corner of Liverpool, new apartment blocks along Shepherd Street cluster around a long, low industrial building – Australia's first paper mill, now housing a smart cafe. Walking through this zone, you're briefly in a model urban future, with the serene gardens and stylish façades of an 'artist's rendition' of how a life is lived. 'It's very funny to see a twenty-storey skyscraper here. My auntie lived in one of the old units.' Speed Street, around the corner, is a more familiar kind of streetscape, lined with mid-rise flats from the 1960s and '70s. Here we're entering phases of Max's characters' lives. Helen, whose story runs through both *The Magpie Wing* and *Paradise Estate*, migrates from junior football to punk and alternative scenes – not unlike Max himself. She avoids her turbulent home life in the suburbs by taking up with twenty-five-year-old mechanic Jeff, staying over at his Speed Street unit two nights a week:

> When he left for work, she tidied away his cans and emptied his ashtray like she did at home with her parents' mess. She showered, changed into the spare uniform she brought over in her bag the night before, and began an hour-long walk to school where she lived the same life her classmates did.

At the end of the street you reach the CBD and, around the corner on Bigge Street, the station. From up on the station bridge, peering through the metal grille, you are startled by another scene from the novel, where one of the characters meets an abrupt end. Striding towards you across the river are four pairs of giant concrete legs, piers stranded in the flat waters of Liverpool Weir. They are what's left of a train line serving Holsworthy Barracks, built during World War I by internees. In the way of vast disused military installations, they create a strange atmosphere in the river, among the trees. 'There's something about abandoned things that sets off some weird spiritual feeling in me. I look at it and feel a ghostly presence.' Along the river, lives have been lived, out of sight. 'We bought a kayak off the *Trading Post* and rode it up and down the Georges River. There were quite a few people who used to live along the banks, just through there, for a long time, undisturbed. I felt, I'm not supposed to do this because I'm paddling past people's homes, and they're sitting in a tent, just hanging out with their own little set-up.'

The town centre is a mix of familiar streets, businesses and shops, preserved in accordance with zoning laws that have only recently been relaxed; there are spice shops, greengrocers, a music store. Opposite the station is a legendary kebab shop, Johnny's, and popping up in the streets around are the high-rises seen from the riverside park and a beautiful new library, a circular building with rows of large portholes, named Yellamundie, meaning 'storyteller' in Dharug language. In front of the library is a surprising steam-punkish statue of colonial governor Lachlan Macquarie, founder of Liverpool. His exposed innards are a book, a quill and a compass, his face both cartoonish and real. Dotted around the grid of streets are several pubs; Liverpool was a major stop for travellers to and from Sydney during the nineteenth century. Many have disappeared or been rebuilt; the structure of the New Commercial Hotel survives in close to original form, though it is closed and a tower is about to be built above it. 'Everyone had their pub: none of us, though. Liverpool pubs seemed too scary to us, very intense. Maybe it's about familiarity, a pseudo rural-to-city disconnect.' There was a sense that it was dangerous to go into the 'CBD', but 'except for being pushed around every now and then by a pack of people at the station, nothing dangerous happened'.

On George Street, the sari shops sparkle with sequins in elaborate window displays amid Indian restaurants. Here Max's character Walt sets up the 'NATIONAL OFFICE OF THE OCPL, which stood, to no one but him, for the Only Communist Party in Liverpool'. Walt has returned to the area at an odd moment in Liverpool's history, at the start of the pandemic, renting the office of a former sari importer. With his sister Helen and friend Duncan he has been milling about the inner west for the later stages of his youth, working on building sites, involved in the punk and communist scenes. Back in Liverpool he begins abortive projects, planting flowerbeds and writing to politicians, the strangeness of his situation intensified by the silent shopping streets outside, usually filled with the toing and froing and socialising of local people.

Walt's character dramatises the ambiguities of moving areas within a city rife with tribalism and snobbery. 'When I moved to the inner west,' Max says, 'people were telling me about how hard my upbringing must have been. It was actually pretty good. It was nice – it was a normal life.' For Walt, after first leaving western Sydney, 'he grew aware of a strange evolution in the region's social and cultural capital … He felt the odd sensation of his background coming into vogue, rising in esteem among the inner-city intelligentsia as though anyone from his neighbourhood had transcended an equal and accepted hardship.' Walt flirts with and provokes the inner-city publishing scene, reading out his spam folder at a poetry night and self-publishing a secession manifesto:

We reject the notion of 'Western' Sydney, which is to say that the area is west of what's important. We prefer to insist that Sydney City is east of interesting ... We advocate for a border and fence to prevent the weekend visits for brief and condescending tastes of that culture.

Walt's secession document is received by those around him, even those who sympathise, as problematically exclusionary and Anglocentric, but it expresses something about what it is like to be looked down upon, and then congratulated, for where you grew up.

A ten-minute drive west from the central shopping streets of Liverpool is our final stop, the Liverpool Catholic Club, where Max trained with the LCC Raiders rugby league club as a teenager. 'It's all here. Even the posts are the same – that faded blue and yellow on the crossbar. The canteen, the barbecues, the change rooms are in this block. The noticeboard hasn't been updated since the early 2000s.' Behind glass sits a faded ad for Billy G's Cookie Dough, a staple of fundraising efforts for kids' sports clubs, offering the prize of a dream-holiday package or some dated-looking electronics. 'These were the sheds; here you'd be, an eight-year-old kid with your mouthguard and your boots, walking out across the concrete, thinking, "I'm a real big tough guy."' Years later, as a teenager, 'the crappy little secondary field was where we trained when I was trying to make the Magpies under-sixteen squad'. The Western Suburbs Magpies were based at Campbelltown then, until the end of the 1990s, when they merged with the Balmain Tigers to become the Wests Tigers. 'That's when I sort of gave up on them. It happened when I was twelve or thirteen. How's it supposed to be my team anymore? Why is there orange on the jerseys? That was my introduction to economic rationalisation.

We can't have twelve clubs in Sydney because we want to attract national sponsors – we want to be in the national competition and grow – there were those sort of explanations from my dad or my uncle or my coach.' That break in connection between club and place created a 'dissonance', a feeling that 'nothing represents me anymore, and the beginning of always looking for something else'.

He stuck with rugby league for a time, moving to Wollongong 'to play for a hundred bucks a week and go to uni down there. I broke my wrist, later on my kneecap'. Along the way, following his interests, he was learning his craft. Max describes in a piece for the State Library of NSW how messing about online taught him to write. He entered obscure competitions, in which he wrote wrestling 'storylines' for online publication and press releases for 'fictional rugby league teams', before contributing to music websites and the street press in order to 'score free CDs and gig tickets ... I discovered Sydney's DIY music community, and through punk, hardcore, experimental and garage music, found something that spoke to me.' In his novels, his characters too try to make things happen through collective experiments; the DIY spirit of zines and blogs is present in the gigs in pubs and warehouses – that democratic, open, connected ethos he found in the early internet. A long project came into being: his zine and podcast series on fifty years of underground music, *Barely Human*.

Eventually, during the quiet days of lockdowns, when casual work fell away, his first novel took shape. 'The pandemic hit my bartending and teacher's aide work, my freelance interviewing for an online magazine. It was really stressful for a month or two and then the welfare rate came up, and I could write.' Even in the more solitary mode of writing, he enjoys the connections made through sharing a sense of the underappreciated textures of urban experience. 'Thankfully, a lot of Australian writers want to write local places now. I was really sick of books set in New York and London. Every now and then someone will reach out and say, "I'd given up on fiction for a long time – it was nice to read your book. You wrote about things that are familiar to me."'

A MAGIC TO THE MIRE

KINGS CROSS, DARLINGHURST AND SURRY HILLS

WITH NEAL DRINNAN

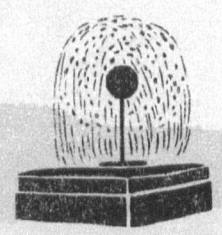

> The street's glamour is its people, not its architecture – girls and boys strutting, preening and drinking. The boys roam from bar to bar, every muscle of their beefcake bodies accentuated by their child-sized T-shirts. Wind-up boy dolls who know instinctively how to move when they hear the doof, doof of that music ... come Saturday night, gay or straight, no one wants to miss out on the show.
>
> – Neal Drinnan, *Glove Puppet*

Between the El Alamein Fountain in Fitzroy Gardens and the Coke sign drawing the curious up William Street lie the storied streets of Kings Cross. For generations, from the days of bohemia and sly grog, through the flows of American servicemen, to the fabulous drag shows of the 1970s onwards, the area has been a magnet for artists, adventurers, lost souls and crims. Through the suburbs fanning from its centre, the Cross's pulsing energies have radiated, luring in many a seeker with their steady beat.

Writer Neal Drinnan spent his early writing years in the suburbs of the inner east, and his Sydney novels of the 1990s and 2000s – *Glove Puppet*, *Quill* and *Izzy and Eve* – tell of dazzling Mardi Gras moments and the high-wire lives of artists, dancers and writers amid their triumphs and falls from grace in the terraces, apartments and bars of gay Sydney. These novels formed the foundation of a writing career spent laying out the dynamics of power, scandal, repression and liberty that shape his characters' lives, and conjure a place and time in the evolution of Sydney's LGBTQIA+ history when a community was claiming visibility and expressing a bold and often glittering form of joy.

By the watery dandelion of the El Alamein Fountain, recent history flickers from the apocalyptic façade of the block that housed the once-roaring Bourbon and Beefsteak twenty-four-hour pub and the drag venue Les Girls. Windows above the hoardings are open to the sky; the awnings and shopfronts are lined with the black-and-white images of a glamorous heyday. The fountain, a burst of city enchantment, was where it all began for a Melbourne boy drawn by tales of the less respectable city to the north. 'I was running away to Sydney but only made it to Albury – I didn't have enough money for the train all the way. When I got up here, I was going to go to that fountain and become a prostitute. I'd seen it on *Today Tonight*, that that's where they worked, and I thought, "Oh, I'm fifteen. I could make a living for myself." Thank god I never got to Sydney.' A few years later, his forays extended, and he hung about here on visits, talking to young sex workers, 'just exploring Sydney, as a young, naive, reckless boy'.

Neal finally made the move on New Year's Day 1996, as a marketing manager for Random House, the manuscript of his first novel tucked in his pocket. This was *Glove Puppet*, a scandalous tale of assumed identity and arch betrayal in which the fates of a dancer and a street boy catastrophically entwine. 'Even though I hadn't lived in Sydney, I had set the whole book here. Sydney inspired me as a writer in ways that Melbourne didn't – I wanted to come and have a go at it.'

There's a sense in the Cross that all human life is here, amid the colonial mansions and Art Deco apartment blocks. North of the fountain on Macleay Street, elderly women emerge from smart foyers, and locals and workers nurse coffees and cigarettes. Potts Point felt 'New Yorky' to Neal; he rented his first unit along this street in a 1920s building with 'one of those wooden lifts, like something out of a New York apartment block, with a little seat that you could sit on and gates that you had to shut. The kitchens were really tiny, and you had a little Juliet balcony with harbour glimpses. It was cute, and full of cockroaches.'

At the side of the building, continuing the New York theme, are fire escapes onto the lane leading down to Elizabeth Bay. Down the alley, a steep set of stairs draws you into shadow before depositing you gently into sunlight and greenery at Billyard Avenue, the harbour sparkling between the apartment buildings. A few steps to the south are the beautiful elevated gardens of Arthur McElhone Reserve, Elizabeth Bay House at the rear. Here Neal joined picnics with others making lives and connections in their new city. 'There was a period of the '90s where many writers came to Sydney from Melbourne and Adelaide. Every Saturday morning in those days we'd have lunch on Victoria Street at one of those cafes, sitting on a milk crate having coffee and toasted sandwiches.' Here in the gardens with their thick lawns, carp drift in languid loops around their ponds. Perhaps the fish remember Neal and his friends, spread across the lawn among their dreams. 'They've always been here. It's like coming out of Kings Cross Station and that shoe shop is still there, even after thirty years. These fish can live as long as we do.'

Winding through the hilly, curved streets of apartment blocks, with ferns and trees sprouting from sandstone walls, the suburb feels placid and exclusive, but its lively history thrums from the old hotels on Elizabeth Bay Road. The distinctive 1970s circular Gazebo building still towers at the top of the street, apartments now. The Gazebo bar has a brief but significant cameo in Neal's novel *Quill*. Here the protagonist Blaise, knocked off kilter by his famous ex-lover's thinly disguised memoir of his love life in Sydney, throws caution to the wind: 'He drained the last of his Scotch and followed the stranger to the lift. He'd always had a soft spot for the Gazebo, or the "Gay's a bow" as taxi drivers seemed to call it.' Across the road, the walls of the Sebel Townhouse, also now an apartment building, had their own tales as the Sydney crash pad of a string of celebrities from Lauren Bacall to the Sex Pistols.

There's a distinct change in feel between the hills and gardens of Elizabeth Bay and the noisy arrival of the main drag of the Cross. Neal would walk along Darlinghurst Road to the station for his publishing job: the off-to-the-city workers, then as now, weaving among the slower movements of the people of the street. 'I had longed to inhabit what I thought of as a really interesting, edgy sort of area – but once you immerse yourself in it, once you see working people and people struggling with drug addiction in the morning when you're on the way to work, and then again on the way home, you realise that you can't be objective about the area. You have to be part of it.'

Walking through at night was a different scene again amid the evening thrillseekers and the burly spruikers badgering passers-by into the strip clubs along here, like Porky's, derelict now, its old neon signs still visible above abandoned shopfronts. 'I'd catch the train home from work and stop at the supermarket. One time I had two bags of groceries and one of those big spruikers – they always seemed to have Cockney accents – said: "Come on, mate. You wanna see some pussy?" I said, "I've got two bags of groceries and people for dinner at eight o'clock. Do I look like I want to –" "*Fuck off!*" he said.' In those early days in Sydney, Neal stumbled across the borders of the darker world around the Cross. 'I got into very scary situations. There used to be these terrible hotels where people were effectively rented by the hour. I'd find myself amid these awful scenes, thinking, "What have I walked into? My god, why would I ever think of buying marijuana here?" There was a lot of darkness.'

Since the 1970s, the Coke sign at the top of William Street has marked the cross of Kings Cross and the gateway to the area. Across the intersection and border with Darlinghurst towers a temporary World Pride installation, *Still Thriving* by Dylan Mooney: a mural of two young Indigenous men embracing amid a rainbow ribbon, wattle flowers and the Aboriginal flag. From here a stroll down Victoria Street takes you past the spot where the stools and milk crates of Bar Coluzzi spilled onto the street for decades, where cyclists, judges, old Italian men and hungover partygoers democratically mingled. Across the road there's the Tropicana Caffe where the Tropfest short film festival began in 1993, and further along, for hearty Austrian fare, there's Una's Restaurant, 'where you could always get a good feed', and still can.

Towards the southern end of Victoria Street is Green Park, squeezed between St Vincent's Hospital and the National Art School, a dense historical site of pleasure, tragedy and memorial. The sandstone-block wall of the art school, formerly Darlinghurst Gaol, runs along the park and down to Oxford Street. 'The Wall' was a gay beat, brought into being by anti-homosexuality laws and perfectly positioned for the traffic between the clubs of Kings Cross and Oxford Street. With the arrival of AIDS in the early 1980s, a 'circle of life and death formed here around St Vincent's Hospital and the Hospice and The Wall, where boys plied their trade from the 1960s'. In this park too the AIDS Candlelight Memorial rallies had their starting point; the historian Gary Wotherspoon writes that 'Many of us remember leaving Green Park for those walks down Oxford Street to the candlelight rallies in Hyde Park, pausing at the hospice to say hello to friends there, out on the balcony.'

'As a twenty-year-old' on his early visits to Sydney, Neal recalls that 'walking along here was thrilling and dangerous. Now I can see what it laid to waste.'

On Oxford Street the rainbow crossing and flag welcome you to Taylor Square. This is a major site in the 'Golden Mile' that stretched from The Albury, just beyond St Vincent's, to Hyde Park, packed in its glory days with pubs and clubs where the community made its own colourful world amid the hostility of the wider culture. Tucked behind Oxford Street on the north side is the curved red turret of the old Darlinghurst Police Station, where protestors at the first Mardi Gras rally of 1978 were locked up and beaten in tiny cells, their names and addresses published the following day in the *Sydney Morning Herald*. The building now houses Qtopia, a museum and advocacy centre that tells the stories of the LGBTQIA+ community in Darlinghurst: police brutality, the devastation of AIDS, but also its creativity, resistance and capacity to celebrate.

The most famous of the community's celebrations is the Sydney Mardi Gras, born of that resistance, running annually along Oxford Street from Hyde Park to Moore Park, and the festival leading up to it. Neal played a part in 'the phenomenon and organisation of turning a social and protest movement into a glamorous international draw' as part of the Literature Committee, producing anthologies of gay writing with mainstream publishers amid a surge of interest among publishers and readers. For two years in a row, during the festival they gave away 20 000 literature samplers of the full-length anthologies, *Fruit Salad* and *20 & Lit*. At Mardi Gras HQ in Erskineville, 'there were all sorts of political dramas and arguments, but through the energy of people in their various arenas – performance art, literature, crowd control, set-building – what they pulled off was incredible'. There was an infusion of corporate money in queer culture, 'a realisation that gay and lesbian stuff was a commercial commodity. All that pink-dollar publishing came on the back of *Priscilla* and Tim Conigrave's *Holding the Man*, as well as authors like Christos Tsiolkas and Fiona Kelly McGregor.' In a sign of that pink dollar's significance to travel and culture, Neal was commissioned during those years to write *The Rough Guide to Gay & Lesbian Australia*.

For Neal, the Darlinghurst stretch of Oxford Street is alive with memories of book launches and significant encounters. Neal had his first launch, for *Glove Puppet* – along with 'unimaginable pre-launch anxiety' – at Stonewall, and in 2006 launched *Izzy and Eve* at The Midnight Shift nightclub. 'Interesting name, "Midnight Shift", as though we shift into something else when the clock strikes twelve, which I suppose we did.' Kinselas, occupying a prominent corner block on Taylor Square and painted now with colourful animal prints, was the site in the late 1990s of Neal's 11 am vodka with the late *Star Observer* columnist and Viper Room compere Lance Leopard, in a meeting to discuss Lance's memoirs. 'He opened an old leather satchel filled with pages of scrawl. "I refuse to use computers," he told me. Even his weekly column had to be transcribed by the receptionist at the *Star*. Each year he published a list of Darlinghurst's twenty-five most beautiful people. I was number seventeen in 1999!' When Lance and his entourage – drag queens, artists, party-types – graced Neal's launches he felt himself for a dazzling moment to be at the heart of gay culture. 'To be famous for a moment is exciting, but even when it was happening it wasn't like it was real – it's all like a dream.'

Just off Taylor Square, a few shops east on Oxford Street, is queer-lit institution, The Bookshop Darlinghurst. Founded in 1982 by Les McDonald, two years before homosexuality was decriminalised in New South Wales, it imported material from the American gay presses in the days before the internet and ready access to queer content. It has championed LGBTQIA+ books and films ever since, providing visibility and promotion to writers from within the community. Les has recently retired (the bookshop is owned now by Charles Gregory, who worked there part-time as a student) but is behind the counter on the day of the walk, as is Graeme Aitken, long-term manager and buyer, and himself an author. In a prominent spot on the wall, a generously sized coffee-table book sports a frank photograph of a bulging pair of underpants. 'I see *The Big Penis Book* is still selling well,' Neal notes. 'Some things the internet can't replace.'

Graeme, like Neal, started writing in the 1990s. 'I published some short stories with BlackWattle Press, the gay and lesbian small press, and then I wrote a novel set in New Zealand.' This novel was *50 Ways of Saying Fabulous*, a funny and charming story about a young boy obsessed with theatre and *Lost in Space* growing up on a remote farm. A moment was happening: 'Australia followed the US, because the US got very excited about gay and lesbian books. They were publishing a lot, with big advances. It was a very exciting time.' These days the publishing energy is around 'trans, non-binary and diverse voices. Hopefully that will endure.'

Graeme first came to work at the bookshop in the early 1990s. 'This whole strip was very lively, and then we had the Albury further down – there were all these warehouse parties every weekend.' And you could move stacks of books if they appealed to the community. 'We sold well over 2000 copies of *Holding the Man*,' he remembers, as well as 1000 copies of *Finding Out*, Paul Freeman's 1997 biography of the first rugby league player to come out, Ian Roberts, and a similar quantity of Graeme's second novel, *Vanity Fierce*. 'The bookshop was always a destination, especially for interstate visitors, and it still is.' The diversification of the queer-lit scene has been a feature of the book industry over the years the bookshop has been in operation, and social movements like Black Lives Matter bring waves of interest and customers through the door.

Back on Oxford Street, it's quiet these days as the strip waits for building projects to complete and the annual spark of Mardi Gras to relight the old Golden Mile. A triple-block laneway development across the road promises culture, food and entertainment, but in a characteristically Sydney turn of events construction has for now halted upon the unearthing of Busby's Bore, a tunnel that supplied water from the Lachlan Swamps in what is now Centennial Park to the colonial city.

Heading down from Oxford Street towards Central Station are the steep streets of Surry Hills, where Neal lived for many years. In the lanes behind Crown Street are rows of intact terraces, a tiny rust-roofed cottage on Reservoir Lane calling up the crowded Surry Hills lives of Ruth Park's *Harp in the South* novels. Above the corrugated roofs shine the tower blocks of the city, ten minutes' walk away. Neal was living in this hilly warren in the late 1990s when he began publishing his own work and producing anthologies for Mardi Gras. On an April night in 1999, half a million hailstones as big as tennis balls rained from the sky, one of them crashing through Neal's skylight and into the dinner on the stove. In *Quill*, Blaise dramatises the famous Sydney hailstorm as a personal attack:

> At once, it was upon him, a thundering sound unlike anything he'd ever heard. Then the glass. First one west-facing window shattered, then another, as if someone were firing a gun through them – a terrible homophobic

siege. Smash, clang, patinck. All he could hear was glass breaking and the din of a thousand car alarms in an apocalyptic symphony.

Further down the hill was Neal's next house in Commonwealth Street, also at the mercy of Sydney elements, its deep gully prone to flooding. He would be out on the street 'in a raincoat trying to stop people from coming past in their cars, because they'd send waves of water into the houses'. The house itself 'had the most revolting bathroom I've ever had, but it became an incredible meeting place and short-term residence for friends, a salon in its own little way'. Neal's local, our last stop on the walk, was the Hollywood Hotel, a classic Sydney corner pub on Foster Street, owned for several decades from the 1970s by actress Doris Goddard, a beloved friend to artists and homeless people. She died in 2019 after many years of singing and telling stories in her bar. 'She played her own compositions, folk songs about meeting someone on a tram to Bondi – she was a bit of a Joni Mitchell character.' There was always anticipation about whether she might come down and sing: 'a significant blessing'.

During this period, Neal wrote the last of his Sydney novels, *Izzy and Eve*. Surry Hills is reimagined as 'the Gilgal', the part of town 'populated with artists, migrants, itinerants and whores'. For all its grit, the appeal is clear: for a city's dreamers and adventurers, 'it's the part of town where round pegs don't have to fit in square holes'. Amid these familiar streets of Chinese rooming houses, taxi drivers lining the street outside the mosque and a backpacker hostel crowded with young hedonists, a city of dark mystery arises. 'The cobbled lanes that run like clotted arteries behind our abodes were once used by night-men who emptied the festering latrines under the discreet cloak of night. Now the same lanes attract alcoholics, drug addicts, pigeons and feral cats.'

In spite of gentrification, traces remain of the neighbourhood's old life: its histories, dangers and intrigue – that old lure of possibility in the heart of the big city. As Neal writes of the fictional Gilgal, there's a lingering sense, as you walk these streets, that 'nothing's changed, yet there's a magic to the mire'.

FEEL EACH PART OF YOUR FOOT ON THE GROUND

BRONTE AND CLOVELLY

WITH BETH YAHP

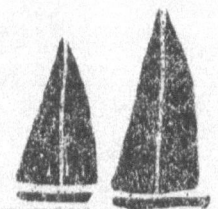

We eat our eggs and toast, then walk my landlady's dog slowly out to look at the sea off the Clovelly cliffs – azure – and we huddle side by side on the wintry rocks in warm sunshine and a cold wind, our backs to the car park. We watch the surf froth around the rocks, rise and fall in white-bearded swoops around Wedding Cake Island. A troop of new divers frog-walks their gear to Gordons Bay. The dog scrambles over the rocks after some seagulls, stops short too close to the cliff edge, leaning into the wind. Ears blown back.

– Beth Yahp, *Eat First, Talk Later*

Tucked away above Bronte Gully is a cut-through between the houses, a hidden lane where greenery spills over the garden fences and crowds the path. After rain, the plants smell fresh, and lorikeets and magpies celebrate the abundance. The walls are painted with butterflies and flowers, ferns sprout from bottles hanging on the fence. These beach suburbs, not far from the city, are generally associated with their breathtaking ocean views and the expensive property blanketing the hills and headlands, but this walk begins somewhere less spectacular, more in tune with the daily pleasures of life. Walking along the lane towards the gully, the vegie beds, street library and scattering of little chairs, tractors and diggers tell a story of a community gathering to plant, tend, play and imagine.

In the work of writer and teacher Beth Yahp, these small moments and pleasures are often where the true story lies. In her memoir *Eat First, Talk Later*, Beth explores the political history of her birthplace Malaysia on a personal scale – through family memory, in recollected meals, through conversations with her parents. Threaded through the memoir too are the moments of her life here in these suburbs by the sea, the clifftop path where she walked Clodagh, her landlady's huge, sweet, temperamental dog, the long cement bathing channel where she nearly drowned, the row of pastel-coloured shops where she worked through the strands of personal and political history among a village of writers, artists and activists.

We're headed from Beth's current neighbourhood, through the lane and down through the gully, via the beaches and cliffs of Bronte and Waverley Cemetery, for Clovelly. 'That's the area I most associate with writing, and thinking about writing. For those of us who do a big creative project, that part of your life is quite distinctive afterwards in your memory. It's connected to place – for me, the last set of shops in Clovelly before the beach.' Here Beth lived for a time in the home of writer, social commentator and activist Anne Deveson. 'Anne found this old butcher's shop that she made into her home. There were street breakfasts, and people going constantly in and out of each other's houses. Anne, as the village elder, would go to all the different places on her rounds. The conversation was always about politics or art or writing – it was wonderful.'

At the end of Palmerston Avenue, the gully reserve plunges down towards the beach through shady bush and ferns, past a red-brick apartment building, with the sound of birds calling through the trees and a waterfall running into the valley. An errant branch reaches across the footpath as you descend; fig roots spread along the rugged sandstone walls. Beth, who has called many places home, finds the tree ferns and lushness remind her of the gullies of the Blue Mountains, and that these places where 'nature has its own ideas' restore a sense of equilibrium after a day spent amid the demands of work and life. 'Sometimes in more urban-dominated areas you feel in control of your environment. Somewhere like this that's allowed to run a little bit wild – even though it's quite designed – nature escapes your intentions. It's so important to feel a different rhythm, an other-than-human pace. The plants grow slowly, we see and smell the regeneration – the earth's just doing what it's doing. You spend all day being weighed down by other stuff, and then you come back and the ground absorbs it.'

The healing properties of green places in the city call to Beth's mind a story from her mentor and friend, the writer Drusilla Modjeska, recounted in an essay for *Meanjin*. 'Drusilla was hosting some Ömie Artists from Papua New Guinea the first time they came to Sydney and they went shopping at the mall to buy things to take back to the village. One of the elders said that she had lost her spirit by the escalators – it was a serious thing. She became really ill. She asked Drusilla: "Where is your ground? We need to go to your ground." So they went for a few turns around the oval and she was restored a little.'

Beth's connection with Drusilla is one of the writerly friendships that has formed the mesh of her community in Sydney since migrating from Malaysia in the 1980s. 'I turned up in her first-year creative writing class at UTS, when it was the New South Wales Institute of Technology back in the mid-eighties. It was astounding to me after the dominance of exams in Malaysia – courses with no grades! The teachers were exceptional. The poet Susan Hampton was another. She taught me about sound and the senses in writing. She taught me about editing – what she called "scalpel" – and "listening like a poet". Drusilla made the idea of a writing life possible – even within reach if I wanted it.'

The enclosed world of the gully opens out to the broad green park, the beach stripes of yellow and blue. At Christmas the grass is blanketed with picnickers celebrating the pleasures of sun and sea; at other times there's a gentler hubbub. Surfers dot the aquamarine waves, swimmers cluster in the shallows. 'Sometimes you see the ocean swimmers from Bondi passing Bronte on their way to Wedding Cake Island at Coogee.' We are happy to enjoy the pleasures of the day from the shore, safe from the 'Bronte Express' – the fierce rip that surfers love. Beth's family lives in Hawaii now, where beach-goers must also maintain proper respect for the ocean. Beth passes on 'that wise Hawaiian adage: never turn your back on the sea'.

At the south end of the beach, the path leads past the Bogey Hole, a sheltered swimming spot enclosed by rocks, and then up above Bronte Baths, jutting out beneath the sculpted white-and-orange layers of sandstone cliff. Until 1960 the Bronte tram used to clatter and ding down the hill here between high sandstone walls, emerging to the spread of blue. The path south takes you through this dramatic cutting up to the green plateau of Calga Reserve, the pale gravestones of Waverley Cemetery scattered across the hillslope ahead.

These cliffs mark the return home from travels near and far. When you fly into Sydney over this rugged coast, 'there's a moment where you feel like you're too close to the rooftops and the water, but somehow you survive'. After a day in the city, driving down into these suburbs, 'there's a hill before you descend to the coast, where the ocean glitters at the end of the road and you know you're almost home. You're descending into something else.'

This path is part of the long chain of tracks, continuous for good stretches, that leads from Manly around the harbour and down the eastern beaches. On any given day these paths skirting the shores of Sydney are lively with walkers, moving at different paces and for different purposes. Beth enjoys the opportunity this place offers for the deliberate slowness of walking. 'There's a writing exercise we give students: a "slowing down" exercise. I first read Jan Cornall's powerful version and adapted it for a writing tour I took to Nepal, a "climbing and writing" journey. You slow down your walk to the point that you feel each part of your foot on the ground, and it forces you into a different experience of time. The world becomes different. When you're out of car time or work time or city time, you're in this other space. Walking does that, because of your connection with the ground – because you notice it.' Beth sees paying close attention to one's own interactions with the world as continuous with the practice of writing. She has said that the task is to 'try to give equal attention to whatever I'm doing – whether it's writing, teaching, editing, or wandering the streets of Manila or Paris, or cooking or eating – writing and publishing new works are part of this larger process, and often not the main part'.

Beth is a great traveller, and walking is also a mode of encounter, of 'saying hello to the place. You see things very differently when you're walking. When I arrive in a place it's about orientation. I remember going to Manila as part of a writing residency, staying in an area that was "dangerous for people who look Chinese", because you can get kidnapped – that was the advice I got. Everybody was saying to me: never, ever walk. It was a private university that had armed guards with metal detectors because people had guns. It was safe and quite rich, and right outside the doorstep across the street from my apartment was this semi-slum area. They had the best markets, I loved it. That kind of walking is about being open to a different sense of time, of being open to a different intention. It's about reading a space that is also reading you.'

At the entrance to the nineteenth-century cemetery, where many Victorian and Edwardian headstones and graves survive intact, is a sign that reads 'Waverley Cemetery: Bidjigal,

Birrabirragal and Gadigal Country', allowing you to pause before entering, to consider a different timescale, an older presence in this place. A wide variety of stone and marble crosses, statues and crypts spills down the grassy slope towards the cliff edge, yellow flowers sprinkled between the plots, the grassy paths worn by feet. Beth notes the many angels; a delicately sculpted, human-sized angel with long curved wings holds his head in his hands above the blue horizon. 'It's good feng shui for the graves here. They have their backs to the hill and they're facing the open sea. It does always feel a bit weird walking through cemeteries, although this is a beautiful one. In Malaysia, we wouldn't go for a stroll through a cemetery without a sense of the things that might linger and follow you home.'

Walking along the paths between the graves, you must decide whether to focus attention on the details all around – the names and dates, the curious crypts and sculptures through which we remember people – or to succumb to the blue immensity of the ocean. Beth holds an affinity, as she writes in her essay 'Small Pleasures', for what the French writer Georges Perec called the 'infraordinary' – 'that which we generally don't notice, which doesn't call attention to itself, which is of no importance'. Walking amid the headstones, Beth notes the ornamentation on a marble column, intricately crafted to look like fabric, and a little bird singing somewhere, for a moment the only sound. Her writing too pays attention to the details through which we know the world, through her practice of writing 'small pleasures'. 'It's about slowing down time, honouring places and things and thoughts and feelings that get overridden by larger things, by the spectacle. The project has been going on for a long time: it's a way of trying to be and stay alive in spaces that can be hostile and consuming, spaces that bury creative endeavour in administrivia or demands to "publish or perish". The idea of "Small Pleasures" started out as a twenty-minute practice, once a day, to write something without thinking, something short and sharp, about a pleasure – no complaining. Some days it seemed impossible, then something pleasurable often arrived, even if only the pleasure of putting words together.'

Back on the path beyond the cemetery is the Clovelly headland with a view south to Coogee and Wedding Cake Island, where memories of previous walks return. 'This is where I used to walk Anne's dog, which was such a big part of my life at that time. She was an Irish wolfhound mix, a softie, but so strong. She was a rescue dog, who'd been brutalised as a puppy. Anne chose her because she was such a funny-looking beautiful dog. Her name was Clodagh. She needed a lot of exercise, she was so big, so I used to walk her twice a day.'

Up ahead, the next bay is Clovelly, with its unusual concrete platforms, built during the Depression to provide local employment as well as better access for swimming. The parallel bathing decks line a long channel of water where you can swim laps or snorkel and look for the latest version of Bluey the groper. The sight of the 'cement beach' conjures a moment that appears in Beth's memoir: 'At that little reef there I was gamely swimming with my partner. I don't swim that well because in Malaysia they say, "Don't swim, you'll get conjunctivitis, you'll drown and die, so better not." I'd been snorkelling a fair bit, in terror. I'm a really weak swimmer. I followed him out over the reef. He caught a wave in, he had flippers and I didn't. I couldn't get back in – I just sank. I could see the bubbles above my head. He came back out and swam me in.' Clodagh, afterwards, was a comfort. Beth writes in *Eat First*, 'Later, at home, squatting hunched over a bucket, I retch up mouthfuls of salt water, while my landlady's large yellow wolf-hound clicks her way across the wooden floor to rest her hairy chin on my back.'

It's a short walk from the beach along a shady green path and the bright street to the little row of shops on Burnie Street, our final stop. Here an old buttery-yellow butcher's shop, the final home of Anne Deveson, sits on the corner of a row of pastel-coloured 1920s houses and shopfronts. Anne was a significant figure in Australian writing, broadcasting and activism, whose life, like Beth's, gave her access to larger stories. Her book *Tell Me I'm Here* told the story of her son's schizophrenia, a cause for which she advocated, and her wartime childhood informed a life of human rights work, as recounted in *Waging Peace*. Anne was also, as Beth describes her, the 'hugely proud' mother of the novelist Georgia Blain, who almost unimaginably died three days before Anne of a brain tumour, in 2016.

Beth and Anne had their Malaysian beginnings in common – Anne was born to a British family in Kuala Lumpur, leaving for Australia during World War II – and when they first met in Western Australia they shared memories of the nuns who ran the convents in Malaysia. 'I'd written a novel, *The Crocodile Fury*, full of Irish and French nuns in Malaysia, and Anne got in contact with me – we were both on writing residencies in Perth. I didn't recognise her. She'd been a journalist with the ABC but apparently people still knew her as "the Omo lady" from a popular ad for laundry detergent in the 1960s. She laughed about that.'

Later, in Clovelly, Anne was Beth's landlady, offering her a home – a grounding – after Beth returned to Sydney from Paris. When Beth was ready to leave, she didn't go far, just across the street. 'What was wonderful about living here was that it really was a village, and Anne was the village elder. Her superpower was connecting people.' They formed a writing group with playwright and poet Alison Lyssa and biographer and fiction writer Barbara Brooks, all working through the questions and challenges of finishing their creative doctorates and of living writing lives. Anne would talk about her memories of the Sydney women's movement, 'how she'd go to consciousness-raising meetings with fiery young feminists in her matching tweeds and think: "Oh, I'm a bit out of place here!" But in her usual fashion she dived into everything with equal amounts of curiosity and enthusiasm – it's what I loved about her.' It eventually became clear though, that Anne was in the early stages of Alzheimer's. 'At one of our writers' workshops, before her diagnosis, she described what it was like: the edges of her mind like cliffs, shearing off, and the blackness remaining. Even then, and later, she was producing incredible metaphors.'

On the quiet shopping street, Beth considers the sunny house where she lived with Anne and Clodagh: 'writers, artists and activists passing through, friends and family, former students, lovers and colleagues, tradie friends and a posse of rescues' like Clodagh, and Beth, 'to whom Anne opened her arms and her home. It was full of talk, laughter, people telling stories, ideas flying around – like Anne's plans for a workshop on flirting … Anne loved yellow. I still have such a strong sense of the vibrant walls outside and the welcome Anne made within. The front part of the shop was her office, where she wrote, surrounded by floor-to-ceiling bookshelves, at a big wooden desk. I wrote upstairs and our writing group gathered at the kitchen table. Those were happy times, even holding sadnesses like Anne's encroaching illness.'

Along with attentiveness, pleasurable smallness and slowing down, Beth counts such places as invaluable in the life of a writer – even if the full realisation comes later. 'Maybe we don't only write with our technologies – our pens, pages, devices

– but with our bodies in space, our conversations and glances, breathing together in the same place.' Those who enable these creative environments, like Anne and all those who entered and enlivened their corner of the village in Clovelly, are intrinsic to the practice of writing. 'For me, writing isn't just what's made on a page or screen. It's about making vibrant welcoming spaces, and the people who come along with you.'

CREATING A LIBRARY

BANKSTOWN AND
PUNCHBOWL BOYS' HIGH SCHOOL

WITH MICHAEL MOHAMMED AHMAD

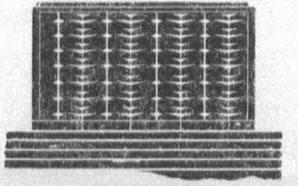

I will take your weightless body from her grip and hold your head, which blazes like the birth of a brand-new star, across my arms. I will tell you about your great-grandfather's arms, which carried his eleven children through the streets of Tripoli and Beirut; and I will tell you about your grandfather's arms, which carried his six children through the streets of Alexandria and Newtown and Redfern; and perhaps one day you will tell your son about my arms, which will carry you through the streets of Lakemba and Punchbowl and Bankstown, where the Arabs will ask me, 'Your son?' and I will reply, 'No, my sun.'

– Michael Mohammed Ahmad, *The Other Half of You*

On Bankstown City Plaza on a cool clear morning, the pretty row of Art Deco shop tops dips away down the hill and people pass by on their way in and out of the station, huffing into their scarves, hands in pockets. There's a quiet hubbub of locals going about their business between Saigon Place, Bankstown Central and the train station. The pace feels gentle, the scale of the buildings manageable, except perhaps for the brightly coloured tower of Western Sydney University's Bankstown campus, visible from a good distance as you approach by car or train.

Michael Mohammed Ahmad, author of the autobiographical novels *The Tribe*, *The Lebs* and *The Other Half of You*, is the founding director of Sweatshop, a literacy and literature organisation working with diverse Western Sydney writers. People from all over the world have made lives here, their children going on to forge their own identities amid the pressures of the wider culture. This walk, on which Mohammed regularly takes local, interstate and international university students, visits sites that for him express the political narratives of this history.

Just a few steps west of the station is the Vietnamese Boat People Monument, a sculpture of a boat containing refugees. Many Vietnamese settled in the south-west of Sydney from the mid-1970s, after the Vietnam War, and this sculpture sits at the top of the street known now as Saigon Place. Mohammed notes the language of the plaque accompanying the sculpture: *Thank you Australia and its people for accepting and supporting the successful settlement of Vietnamese people.* 'That's an interesting angle, because it's the Vietnamese thanking Australia, as opposed to the other way around.' Mohammed talks about the seminal work of social theorist Ghassan Hage, *White Nation*, in which Hage finds that White Australia holds 'a "fantasy position" of dominance. It's a fantasy of being the master and facilitator of the nation. Migrants and First Nations people are imagined as objects to be governed. This is a good example of the white-nation fantasy: the Vietnamese are thanking Australia for their permission to be here, even though it was Australia that participated in the illegal invasion of their homeland.'

As we walk north along the plaza past the station, Mohammed indicates the people milling about. 'If you look around Bankstown, it's just a happy, vibrant community. It's middle class, but it's very diverse – not a white, gentrified middle class. The communities themselves became middle class over the decades.' Multiculturalism is not something to 'do away with, or embrace' as a policy by a political party, he says. 'It makes no difference to the reality of Australia, which is diverse whether the policy-makers accept that or not.' He notes that a large number of locals will be fasting for Ramadan, as he is himself. Easter is not long past, and so at this time in the area 'there's this really beautiful moment of community and interfaith dialogue going on'.

There's a garden on the north side of the station with benches where you might find a quiet moment amid the coming and going, although the cockatoos screech wildly. Here there is a plaque for a schoolboy, Omar El-Chami Batch, who died in 2001. 'Remember the hysteria around Bankstown and the western suburbs, particularly around Vietnamese and Arab communities?' At that time, in the popular press, certain suburbs of Sydney – Bankstown among them – became synonymous with gang violence. Mohammed recounts the context for the killing of Omar, the turf wars of that time and its innocent victims. 'On the spot where we're standing – this used to be a bus stop – was a boy I went to school with: Omar El-Chami. He was a really good boy. He was studying. He wanted to be an engineer.' Omar was waiting for a bus when he was shot three times by people identified as members of a Vietnamese gang, and died of a heart attack. 'It was believed that the random assault on Omar's life was revenge for the murder of an innocent Korean-Australian boy named Edward Lee some months earlier in Punchbowl, by members of a "Middle Eastern gang".'

From the plaque, Mohammed reads: 'In memory of Omar El-Chami Batch, age sixteen years, 24-10-1984 to 16-2-2001. An innocent bystander who tragically lost his life, remembered by family and friends. RIP.' There is Arabic script on the plaque; 'It asks you to recite the fatiha – the opening of the Qur'an – for Omar's spirit. B-ismi-llāhi r-rahmāni r-rahīmi … ' In the name of Allah, the Most Gracious and the Most Merciful. Mohammed was at home after school as the news came through that a boy had been shot in Bankstown, but no one knew who it was at that stage. 'I remember my dad saying, "Find your brother." We spent hours trying to call him.

We were very worried.' Mohammed's brother eventually surfaced, and the news spread that it was Omar, from their school. 'It was a very hard time for our community. I did lose a brother; we *all* did. There was so much anger. There was desire for revenge. But Omar's mother called for peace and forgiveness.'

As a young Arab boy growing up in the area, Mohammed was used to negative stereotypes. The Muslim male, he says, was a kind of folk devil. In the midst of media narratives connecting gang wars and sexual violence with ethnicity, the September 11 attacks occurred, revivifying tropes of the Arab terrorist. 'You would be seen as a drug dealer, a terrorist, a sexual predator – and you'd be moving in and out of those categories in your day-to-day life.' Mohammed's novels follow an alter ego, Bani Adam, through many of these episodes. Bani's years as a teenager amid this febrility are covered in the second book, *The Lebs*. '"Lebs" is not shorthand for "Lebanese",' Mohammed explains. 'It's a term that emerges in Western Sydney during this period of the folk devil. It's a brand-new identity – a uniquely Australian identity. It has elements of Arab-ness in it – language, cultural practices, foods you eat, particular mannerisms, hand gestures – that come from the Arab world, but it also has a type of underclass Australian-ness that you would find among all Australian men whether they're working class or upper class, whether they're white, whether they're black, whether they're brown.'

In the late 1990s in Western Sydney, 'young brown men were appropriating and adopting African American behaviour, specifically gangster rap, Biggie and Tupac, using all the gestures and emulating the music. If you were walking down here twenty years ago, you'd be hearing Tupac blasted all over the place.' These young men identified with the black civil rights struggle, and the music articulated their own experiences. 'We were being demonised by politicians; we were being harassed by police. So this hybrid identity I call "Leb", in addition to Australianness and Arabness, also had elements of African American and Latino subculture and hype.' Mohammed's friends were from Lebanese, Syrian, Palestinian and even Indonesian backgrounds, mixed. 'And yet we all identified as Lebs. It's a kind of unique Western Sydney identity created in response to the demonisation of the community.'

A block north along Fetherstone Street is a wide expanse of park and terraces, lined on the far side by large public buildings, with the mid-century circular council building in the foreground. Through this serene environment, global histories and narratives flow. 'Living in Bankstown, you're in a very specific place and you're in the entire world at the same time. In the time we've been talking we've walked past a hundred people who each speak a different language. Western Sydney has one of the fastest growing populations in the country. Nearly ten per cent of the country lives here. It has the largest population of people who identify as First Nations.'

Here in the corner of the park are reminders of two key figures associated with Bankstown. The park is named for Bankstown boy and former prime minister Paul Keating, and the suburb itself for James Cook's botanist Joseph Banks. Two sculptures in the south-west corner, quite different to one another, commemorate Banks. One, just in front of the circular council building, is a fluid, graceful 1960s sculpture resting in a garden bed: a large female figure holding aloft a plant to represent 'the Spirit of Botany'. But the statue Mohammed points out of Sir Joseph Banks at the junction of Chapel Road and The Mall is in a more traditional style, though more recently installed. 'In addition to having a suburb named after him, there's also the banksia plant, and we have a school named after him in this area, Sir Joseph Banks High

School.' Mohammed notes the 'white Australian hypocrisy and paradox' in naming one suburb of Western Sydney Pemulwuy, after the Bidjigal warrior, and naming this one Bankstown: the botanist, on his return to England, was sent Pemulwuy's head for his collection. His remains have never been returned to First Nations people in spite of continuing requests.

Across the park, the new Bankstown campus of Western Sydney University brings students from the train station five minutes away. The old campus in Milperra was difficult to get to, and it is energising for the city to have students milling about. The scale of the building for Mohammed, though, is something of an adjustment amid the familiar streetscape – twice as big as the council tower next to it, which was always 'this big blue iconic building. It's been quite confronting to drive past the city's new monolith.' As ever, when streetscapes reconfigure, the people of a city make internal rearrangements that force adjustments in memory, a stumble in the flow of internal time and space.

Generally, the university has been a boon for the area. 'It has a very high proportion of kids who are the first in their families to obtain a tertiary education. It's great that the kids are going to be here, and it's really good for the local economy. I was walking past earlier and there's a lecture theatre – look, you're out in the open.' Drawing level with the building, you can see right through into the lecture theatre from the path. 'This visibility of knowledge is important. Take note of the old library.' Across the square towards the city centre is a shut-up building fronted by a row of columns: dark panels with points at the top. 'See how those panels are covering the windows? Old libraries were very inaccessible. The way they built the old library, it's like they barricaded it up. We used to treat knowledge like this sacred thing only a few people could have access to, whereas these new libraries are entirely made of glass and you can see right through them. The knowledge is treated as transparent – something everybody should have access to and should be transferring and sharing.' He sees this idea expressed in the lecture theatre visible from outside the university building. 'The old idea of a lecture theatre is this closed-up room that nobody from the outside world could access. Now there's a lecture theatre where my dad, a sixty-year-old illiterate migrant from Lebanon, can see what's happening while he's walking past on the street. I was the first in my family to go to university. He never could have imagined what I was doing there and what it looked like for me, whereas now these spaces are open for all of Bankstown to see.'

Grand concrete steps lead up towards the new Bankstown Library and Knowledge Centre, built of glass in a modern, eye-catching design. The louvre pattern across the front looks like the kind of stretchy webbing that you might find wrapped around an exotic pear. In front of the library is a wide reflective pool. Passing inside you can see out across the square to the old library through the massive window and intriguing pattern of the louvres. Inside, there's a vertical garden and graceful columns, spreading at the roof.

And then, at the back of the library, behind the children's area, Mohammed reveals a beautifully designed reading garden. Here you can imagine children gathering on the large, smooth, pebble-like stools under the generous shade of the umbrella, or lying dreamily on the deck in the sun, surrounded by prettily landscaped native grasses. Near the door is a bronze sculpture of the poet Kahlil Gibran, accompanied by a plaque: *For the people of Bankstown, in recognition of the contribution of the Australian Lebanese community to our city.* 'It's very different to the way the Vietnamese memorial was articulated. This one is recognising the contribution of the Lebanese community to Australia, rather than the contribution of Australia to the Lebanese community. But the reason why this is such a special garden to me is because of my son – we named him Kahlil. His mother and me both love the Lebanese poet so much that we wanted him to be our son's namesake.' For Mohammed, the poet's name represents unity: 'He's very non-divisive among Muslim and Christian Arabs. *The Prophet* is a text that resonates very much with the Muslim world, even though it was written by an Arab from a Christian background.'

Next it's a ten-minute drive to Punchbowl Boys' High, where Mohammed went to school, with time on the way to talk about Sweatshop. Identifying as Lebanese has been important to Mohammed's feeling of solidarity with local writers from Arab and Muslim backgrounds, 'but I would like to think that my solidarity is broad. Sweatshop is a movement for First Nations people and people of colour.' The organisation bases its foundational motto on the words of social theorist bell hooks, stating on its website: 'We cannot talk about freedom and justice in any culture unless we are talking about mass-based literacy movements.' So many others have spoken on behalf of the community from outside; the potential is in nurturing local voices. 'There are so many hybrid communities here that have not yet been represented. It's like an incubator, a melting pot for stories. There's a library that needs to be created and we're creating it.' He offers a striking example of the unheard voices beginning to break through: general manager of Sweatshop Winnie Dunn's *Dirt Poor Islanders* is the first novel published in Australia by a Tongan writer.

Punchbowl Boys' High School – the cluster of brick buildings, the broad playing field stretching to the train line – is silent for the school holidays. It looks like other public high schools in Sydney: a mid-century two-storey block, a green metal fence around the playing field, a gate at the office. In a piece that Mohammed wrote about the response inside the school to September 11, he describes the place of his youth: 'The school building was surrounded by barbed wires and cameras, which is why we called it Punchbowl Prison.' He says now: 'There's the new Punchbowl and the old Punchbowl. Today they're just regular school fences, but when I was growing up, they were chain fences, twice as high, with barbed wires right through. In most schools, you can walk in and out of the main gates. In this school, you had to go through the front office. It wasn't only about keeping the boys in, it was about keeping intruders out. The number of friends I had who would have some kind of jagged scar from the barbed wire.' There were cameras too, before it was normal to have cameras. 'I came home from school one day and we were on the news. My friends were rattling the gates and telling the journalists they were in jail. The whole news story was about cameras, barbed wires – it was a story about how the boys had been locked in.'

Mohammed credits the transformation of the school to a Lebanese Muslim principal, Jihad Dib, who later became the state Member for Bankstown. 'He'd stand down here, see the kids in the morning, shake hands with all of them, talk to them.' This was a little after Mohammed's time here. Ten years ago, the TV series *The Principal* told the story of a local man trying to transform a terrifying school that seemed modelled on Punchbowl with its barbed wire and unruly boys, a representation Mohammed explores in an essay titled 'Lebs and Punchbowl Prison'. The writers and producers, from outside the community, 'wanted to portray the anti-social history of Punchbowl Boys', but were missing one crucial ingredient: it wasn't as dark, grey and depressing as they made it seem.

The boys come in, they're poking fun. They're laughing. They're not miserable. They don't aspire to be middle-class white kids. They're having a perfectly good time being poor brown kids.'

Passing the school buildings on Kelly Street, Mohammed calls up a scenario: 'You had cameras on this building. You had this huge oval. In the far corner over there, between the train line and the street – that was the only way you could really get out, where the barbed wire ended. So here's what it was like: you would have to get here at just the right time and sprint as fast as you could before the camera caught you on the monitor. And you had to get to that corner and make a break for it – it was a prison break. It was exhilarating. We skipped school quite a lot.' It's a good distance, this diagonal bolt across the field, a couple of hundred metres. In *The Lebs*: 'we are our fastest, we are most united, when we sprint across the oval not to score a try but to break out … my heart pounds like iron and the splints in my shins become shockwaves …' Some of his teachers were not thrilled about the portrayal of the school in his novel, he says. 'But I'm very proud of this place. I'm proud to have been a Punchbowl Boy. It made me.'

Not long ago, the actor Claudia Karvan filmed here for a day with Mohammed for her show *Books That Made Us*. The boys took him to a beautiful cafe they had made in the school. 'One of the boys said to me, "What was it like when you were at this school?" I said to the boys, "I didn't come to this school. Seventy per cent of you go to university now. When you appear in the media it's for things like this, the ABC visiting to tell the story of a student who has done well. But the school I went to, there were few subjects to study, virtually no options. We weren't allowed to go to sports carnivals because we were banned. We regularly saw boys get stabbed in our classes." Watching the space transform over twenty years, it's very special.'

Where might a love of literature have come from? What lit that fire, in such a distracting environment? 'Mum and Dad were illiterate. They came here from Lebanon when they were teenagers. My mum started having kids, my dad worked his heart out, and neither of them finished school. There were no books in my house – my love for books came from their absence. As a kid, I loved words. I loved thought, I loved ideas, and so I remember rummaging through the house and looking for stuff to read, and there was nothing.'

Mohammed was ten when his family moved from Sydney's inner west to Lakemba. 'It was a very exciting time because there were a lot of Lebanese people there – we called it "Leb-kemba". It was the first time we met so many people who looked like us, spoke like us, had names like ours, ate the same food as us, didn't eat certain things that we couldn't eat.' Mohammed's parents had another life-changing transformation in store for him. 'When we moved to Lakemba, my mum and dad said to me: "You're going to be really happy, Mohammed, because there's a library just down the street from where we live." I remember the first day I got to Lakemba, at ten years old. I went down the street and I got my first library card. I spent most of my childhood between those quiet rows of bookshelves.'

'There's something quite unusual about human beings,' Mohammed reflects, standing beside the sports field of his old high school. 'We have this quality in us that no other living creature on this planet has – this desire to read, this desire to develop language. We transfer the most beautiful and complex way of thinking onto the page – that's literature.'

A PLACE OF REVELATIONS

COOKS RIVER

WITH MICHELLE DE KRETSER

> ... the park detached itself from the night. Koels called, and currawongs – the birds who had whistled over his childhood. Fifteen minutes by train from the centre of the city, he lived among trees, birdsong, Greeks. The Greeks, arriving forty years earlier, had seen paradise.
>
> – Michelle de Kretser, *The Life to Come*

The Cooks River, over the course of its life, has altered shape and flow as the eastern swamps and waterways retreated and re-formed with the encroachment of the ocean, and people. On its shore the famed Bidjigal warrior Pemulwuy began his resistance to the colony, spearing First Fleet gamekeeper John McIntyre before escaping through the marshes to fight another day. The river has suffered a rough history in the hands of the colonists, constricted by concrete, poisoned by waste, lost to the swimming and fishing of previous millennia, but the communities on its banks have fought over time to restore it to a healthy system for birds, fish and people. The river is, for long stretches, a beautiful place to walk or lie under a tree, its marshy history evident in its greenery and birdlife.

A section of parklands and golf course runs along the river from Hurlstone Park to Tempe, a trail connecting several suburbs of the inner west. You can walk for hours through this green corridor, barely troubled by traffic. The terrain shifts as you turn corners, follow the river bends, emerge from the trees to encounter local wonders: sandstone cliffs, thickets of mangrove, hidden gardens and, in quiet moments away from the roads and between planes, only the sound of birds. This area – its floods and surprises – is vividly present in the writing of novelist Michelle de Kretser, particularly in *The Life to Come* and *Springtime: A Ghost Story*. A sense is emitted of discovering Sydney from an oblique angle, of it being revealed in glimpses and gulps from unexpected vantage points, by generous hosts who offer these revelations as gifts passed on. A walk along the banks of the river amid the greenery and birds feels like this too: an unveiling of a city secret.

At the Dulwich Hill light rail station, the tracks gleam away into the sandstone cutaways and weedy banks of the inner west. Behind the station is a narrow cut-through. 'In spring this is bougainvillea lane,' Michelle says, describing its seasonal blaze of colour. Down Wardell Road is Marrickville Golf Course, the first stretch of green as you approach the river. Early on a cold winter weekday morning, when the golfers were 'lie-abeds', Michelle used to take her dog Minnie and stride across the terrain. The course has a country-park feel, landscaped but undulating, following the line of the water. 'In winter it's like *Wuthering Heights* – blustery and wild. When the sun's only just up, it's quite magical. I always felt lucky that we had the river.'

Michelle lived in Melbourne – a city of majestic parks – before Sydney, and the rivalry between cities emerged in the comments people made when she moved, playfully recreated in *Springtime*:

> That spring, Frances walked along the river every morning with her dog, Rod. One of the things that had been said in Melbourne when she announced that she was moving to Sydney was, You'll miss the parks. Other things included: There are no good bookshops there. And, What will you do for food.

Michelle's source for the dog Rod was her own much-loved Minnie, who haunts these tracks now that she's gone. 'I used to walk everywhere with her. For a long time after she died, I didn't come back here.' In a piece about this loss, Michelle writes of the distinctive sense of discovering a place with Minnie. 'We saw the sun rise over the wind-blown hills of the local golf course; we took long, picturesque walks along the banks of the Cooks River.' When Minnie grew ill, she began to lead Michelle on strange new paths, and their walks took on the mysterious shapes of her dog desires, leaving the streets and paths now crisscrossed with memory.

On the footpath-climb to skirt the golf course, the village-like nature of Sydney makes itself felt, the way suburbs are enclosed and cut off by ridges and valleys, cliffs and rivers, the tentacles of the harbour. A city's form has an effect on thinking and ways of being. 'Melbourne has these long, flat streets – you can follow a street and end up on the other side of the city with ease. You just glide along.' For the narrator in Michelle's latest novel, *Theory & Practice*, 'the city's endless flat, unkinking streets made me feel as if they might draw me on forever. I wondered whether, if I stayed long enough, my thoughts would stretch, would unroll steadily, without hurry or fret about destination.' Sydney, 'a place of hills and valleys and pockets', here green-sloped, clamorous with birds, releases a different mood. 'Even on a grey day it has its own excitement, its own feeling of being up in the air, up in the world.' The shaded pathways and green stretches remind Michelle of walking in France, where she spent her young adulthood. 'There is nothing more inviting than a grassy track, something incredibly romantic and inviting to the imagination.'

Where Illawarra Road crosses the river towards Earlwood, magpies peck around the picnic benches at the edge of a broad oval. Across the bridge, a bike path bound eastward towards Botany Bay dips down the riverbank. Here are secluded, sometimes lushly overgrown gardens of modest, intriguing houses that conjure for Michelle holiday places in a river town. Trees hang over the path; water glints among the dark mangroves. And then, as you loop back around to the front of these houses on Undercliffe Road, the landscape opens up to the drama of Earlwood's sandstone cliff, houses peeking out above its lip. Green-sprouting driveways lead downwards to riverfront gardens. Ducking down footpaths, emerging into the open, is to experience a sense that Sydney offers 'of secrets, of revelations. That's what Sydney seems to me to be, a place of revelations, because of the hills, because of the topography. You don't know what's coming. Look at that magnificent sandstone cliff with trees growing out of it. It reminds you that you are living in a natural landscape, even though it's profoundly urban.' Delia Falconer's book *Sydney*, Michelle says, gives this feeling of a city whose bones are coming up through the skin. 'The power of this landscape, the sheer age of it: deep time feels close here.'

Back on the river track heading north-west, a cyclist zips decorously around the walkers on the path. The bike traffic is gentle, compared to the peak-hour mayhem of 'managerial types off to sack someone'. A shed in a riverside garden suggests itself as a dreamy writing studio. The trees are alluring: a Queensland hardwood with a brief, spectacular flowering that can be seen from the other side of the river, a cascade of brugmansia trumpets. There's a rundown house, reassuring messiness amid the shiny renovated surfaces and sharp-edged lawns spreading across the surface of the city. Then, unnervingly, in a shady garden, a figure appears, motionless, wrapped in a shawl, an apparition from Michelle's story *Springtime*. 'I was coming along here once on a misty morning with Minnie. It was deserted, except for a lone cyclist coming the other way. He fell off his bike when he drew abreast with this garden, he was so startled.' If you are curious, Michelle's ghost story *Springtime* will introduce you to this enigmatic figure, tucked away in a garden on the banks of the river.

As we head west through Earlwood, Michelle points out Fairway House, a Harry Seidler apartment block just up the hill above Riverview Road, frontage staggered to maximise light and views. The real estate ads make the most of the apartments' dreamy outlook, across the parklands and roofs and trees to the city skyline. As ever in Sydney, the outward appearance of the building divides opinion, while its occupants gaze out at their wonderful view, immune to judgement.

Over here, aside from the units, people live on blocks that are big for the inner west. This area was home to one of Sydney's many quarries and its workers; then, as George Meshaw notes in *The Life to Come*, in the mid-twentieth century, the Greeks found themselves this little paradise. Starting in Marrickville, they spread onto the larger blocks in the surrounding suburbs, other waves of migration following them. This sense of multicultural Sydney is ever-present in Michelle's books; the whole world is in these stories, just as it is in this city, these suburbs. Migrant families' former homes across the world can be seen in the loving features of the houses: Corinthian columns, terrazzo paths, elaborate planters, lemon and olive trees, and rosemary bushes. 'These people often grow pumpkin,' Michelle comments, passing one house, 'down the balconies and over the fence.' Further along the path there is a garden spilling onto public land beyond the property line, with olive trees and rosemary, pumpkin and zucchini. Artist Jacqueline Larcombe, using French philosopher Michel de Certeau's term, names the residents of Earlwood 'artist-inhabitants', who create the Greek textures of this suburb through their acts of tending. Their exuberant gardening adds to the uncontained feel of the land, monstera spreading madly on the shady paths, mangroves creeping into the river, trees twisting from sandstone.

The houses evoke their own dreamlife. In *The Life to Come*, George Meshaw's house is on the other side of the river. 'I saw a white house on one of my very early walks with Minnie. It haunted me, that house, and I put it in *The Life to Come*. And then long after I'd written that part, I went back and found it again. It's completely ordinary – somehow my mind had made it into a much more mysterious and magical space. For me to want to write about it, it had to be transformed in that way.'

A footbridge disappears into thick mangrove; currawongs release their otherworldly cries. On the grassy banks of the river, magpies and ibis seek out morsels across the swampy fields. Walking in Sydney, the birds shriek and chatter over every human encounter. In *Theory & Practice,* Michelle writes of the 'hullaballoo of Sydney' and in *The Life to Come*, Sri Lankan migrant Christabel sits on her St Peters doorstep in the dark with her first cup of tea as the birds start up, 'tuneful, scratchy or liquid conversations, all coiled through with energetic chatter and throaty shrieks'.

Back across the river, via a footbridge at Foord Avenue, is Hurlstone Park, the final stretch of this loop, characterised by the Federation houses that began popping up along the trainline at the turn of the twentieth century. These waves of development continue in the apartment blocks being built around the station, and the new Metro line will bring more change still. The streetscape feels protected here, though – out of time. A wild and grassy cut-through takes you above a playground, overhung by a beautiful gum tree. Old trees crowd out cottages, bikes lean against walls, stairs have been cut from one street to another, gouged out of the craggy rock. 'Hurlstone Park is like this little pocket that time forgot. Some of the houses remind me of growing up in Colombo in the sixties.' These glimpses of other places amid the overgrown shagginess of Sydney flicker continually in Michelle's novels for her diasporic characters. For Christabel, images of Sri Lanka are 'always there, running invisibly under her Australian life'. Another of the novel's characters, Ash, born in Scotland, educated in the UK and the States, has spent a part of his childhood in Sri Lanka, the land of his father. For him, his past and present are brought together on his arrival in Sydney by the smell of the sea, tropical rot and warm light:

> The city smelled briny and fumy ... In those first weeks, when he was at his most porous, past and present fused ... He recognised things he couldn't name: trees that ruined concrete with their toes, reckless floral perfumes. Even the fruit bats rotting on power lines were dreamy visitants from the past. Sydney was a summer city as London was a winter one.

The weather in this city, its sensory evocations, stitches places and times together. 'One of the reasons I love Sydney is that for five to six months of the year it reminds me of Sri Lanka. It has that lushness and warmth.' And for those luscious five to six months, the people of Sydney make the most of their city: New Year's picnics on the harbour, balmy evenings on the ferry out to Manly. 'There's something wonderful about the democracy of Sydney's beaches, that you can't own a beach. The beach is the workers' paradise. I see people picnicking or just resting out on the headlands and think, "How glorious."' The Russian Sydneysider Joseph in *Springtime* offers newcomers Frances and Charlie such gifts, inviting them 'to the opera, to the sea baths at Coogee, to picnics in blossomy parks where hidden steps led to the harbour'. Michelle recalls Christmas picnics at Yurulbin Park in Birchgrove, with views of the Harbour Bridge and plenty of space to spread a blanket, 'no one about but a fisherman on the rocks below because the locals have their own view from their gardens'.

That narrow point reaching out into the harbour from the Balmain peninsula is a part of Sydney many readers will associate with Peter Carey's *Oscar and Lucinda*, an example of one of the pleasures of cities: that their stories are rich ingredients of our imaginative relationship with them. 'The reason we all know London or New York long before we get there is because they are so represented – over-represented – in literature and film and the visual arts. Cities have histories, but they also require mythologies, and that's what literature or art can provide.' When Michelle moved to Sydney, she looked for contemporary books set in the city, and more specifically in the inner west, largely unknown then to literature. There were classics of Sydney's east from Jessica Anderson, Ruth Park and Patrick White, but 'when we first moved here, my part of Sydney wasn't legible to me, because it hadn't already been predigested by other writers and represented in novels. I was sorry that I wasn't over in the east, where I recognised places from literature. But then, of course, I realised it's fantastic – the neighbourhood I live in is there to be written about now.'

ALWAYS HERE

CITY AND REDFERN

WITH
LARISSA BEHRENDT

I remember my grandmother telling me as we passed
the south end of Hyde Park where there was a war
memorial that once upon a time this had been a place
where blackfellas from the southern tribes had met and
camped. There was conflict – violent conflict – between
them and the first settlers. I always thought since then
that we should have a war memorial that honoured our
heroes, our warriors, too.

– Larissa Behrendt, 'Under skin, in blood'

In Hyde Park, the colony's oldest, green amid the rush and concrete, there are wide paths to saunter and a cooling fountain topped with graceful sculptures. Office workers eat sandwiches and peer into their phones under the figs, prehistoric ibis hop onto bins, delving with their long thin beaks for treasure. The sandstone forms of colonial history are all around: to the north are the Hyde Park Barracks, where, from 1819, convicts rose to the clanging of the bell, heading out to nearby Brickfield Hill and the breweries, docks and foundries to build the colonial city. Along the eastern border: St Mary's Cathedral, the Australian Museum and Sydney Grammar School. Within the park, Captain Cook has held his telescope aloft since the late nineteenth century, in spite of recent attempts to cut him down at the ankles, and the southern end of the park is dominated by the pale monument of the 1930s Anzac Memorial and its broad reflective pool.

These monuments and institutions are the work of a moment in the Aboriginal time of this place. Other sites in this part of Sydney open up counter-histories, sites of resistance, centres of collective belonging. Sharing her memories and knowledge of the area is Euahleyai and Gamillaroi woman Larissa Behrendt, a law professor and storyteller who works in many forms – fiction, nonfiction, radio and film. Larissa was raised in Sydney and lives within walking distance of Hyde Park, the community organisations of Redfern, and her workplace at University of Technology Sydney on Broadway. Her walks between these locations take her continually through important sites of personal and collective memory, where the layers of old and recent histories surface, and culture, community and activism continue.

Close to the south-western corner of Hyde Park, within sight of the Anzac Memorial, a striking sculpture glints from amid the trees: seven giant bronze and silver-coloured bullets – four standing, three fallen. The work is called *Yininmadyemi, Thou didst let fall*, and marks the starting point of this walk. 'I like this part of Sydney,' Larissa says. 'There's a hidden history to it. Where the war memorial is now was a meeting place for Aboriginal people coming from the south or displaced from around the Sydney basin. There was a big community that lived here.'

The standing bullets reach towards the sky, miniatures of the city towers beyond. One of the prone bullets is propped against another. 'The other thing here that's important for me is this sculpture by Tony Albert in the shadow of the war memorial – a memorial to the Aboriginal men and women who fought for Australia in the wars. The sculpture is very much about Tony's own family's experiences in combat.' Tony's family is of the Girramay Kuku Yalanji and Yidinji groups of Far North Queensland, and the piece tells the story of his grandfather Eddie's capture by Italian soldiers during World War II. Of this group of seven prisoners of war, three were shot. Here the bullets lie, their companions standing close around them. On their return from war, Aboriginal soldiers like Eddie weren't given land like other returning servicemen; *Yininmadyemi* was made to provide a space for others to tell their stories, and for the wider public to hear them. Larissa has her own connection to this history: 'Both my parents, including my Aboriginal father, served in the armed services. Dad was in the navy and Mum was in the women's navy. It's an important part of our history. This sculpture is so dominant in the landscape. For a history that was forgotten – not in our own families, but by the national narrative – I love that it's this bold, provocative installation that stops people in their tracks.'

The work that Tony Albert and others are making as part of Queensland Aboriginal artist collective proppaNOW, and with Boomalli ('to strike, to make a mark') in New South Wales, is 'part of an arts movement that speaks to my experience, my politics, my generation'. Another proppaNOW member is legendary artist-activist Richard Bell, subject of a recent film directed by Larissa, *You Can Go Now*. Bell's most famous artwork is *Embassy*, an installation that has toured the world: a representation of the Aboriginal Embassy first set up under a beach umbrella on the lawns of Old Parliament House in Canberra on 26 January 1972. Like Tony Albert's *Yininmadyemi*, *Embassy* is a space to tell stories and encounter the truth of colonisation. In its recent home in the Tate Modern in London, the tent installation was paired with Bell's *Pay the Rent*, a huge digital ticker displaying an ever-rising figure.

Here in the park, on the other side of the world, towers the 'notorious sculpture of Captain Cook that still says "discovered in 1788"'. For Larissa, the big bullets of *Yininmadyemi* also reference the older conflict that James Cook's arrival precipitated: 'the frontier wars and resistance in this country'. The location is important, 'here on the site of a displaced camp from the first days of the colony. There has always been resistance from the very first. There have always been Aboriginal people here and always ways in which the community claims this land.'

Crossing Liverpool Street at Museum Station in the southwest corner of the park, you're ejected back into the rumble of the city. Across Elizabeth Street is the old Mark Foy's department store, now the Downing Centre local courts, still bearing the words *SILKS MILLINERY SHOES LACES GLOVES*, and people move to and fro between work and lunch, zipping about in suits and taxis. The everyday bustle underscores the significance of the city's important places for Larissa, where people might walk past, not realising what, and who, is here. 'When I was growing up in Sydney, the usual thing was to say, "There are no Aboriginal people here." There was a real invisibility. Now that we do Acknowledgement of Country, there's a much greater sense of who the traditional owners are. That sense of invisibility is changing, but there are still all these little histories that I love knowing are there.'

Here amid the workaday bustle of the city fringe is an unassuming building with a significant past and present: Australian Hall at 150 Elizabeth Street. 'This was the site of the 1938 Day of Mourning, a very important moment in our protest history.' At a time when Aboriginal people suffered the restrictions of the missions and the injustices of racist laws outside them, the Aborigines Progressive Association, or APA, in New South Wales and the Australian Aborigines' League in Melbourne organised the first national protest. On the 150-year anniversary of the arrival of the First Fleet, they marched silently from Town Hall to Australian Hall, with attendees from the reserves at risk of imprisonment and the loss of their homes and jobs. A photograph of delegates in this very spot depicts a group of women, men and children in dark formalwear standing in front of a sign reading 'Aborigines Conference', holding smaller signs reading 'Aborigines claim citizen rights!' That day, they passed the motion:

> WE, representing THE ABORIGINES OF AUSTRALIA, assembled in conference at the Australian Hall, Sydney, on the 26th day of January, 1938, this being the 150th Anniversary of the Whiteman's seizure of our country, HEREBY MAKE PROTEST against the callous treatment of our people by the whitemen during the past 150 years, AND WE APPEAL to the Australian nation of today to make new laws for the education and care of Aborigines, we ask for a new policy which will raise our people TO FULL CITIZEN STATUS and EQUALITY WITHIN THE COMMUNITY.

This place and its history are alive to Larissa. 'I love that when I'm going to catch the bus, I walk past these steps. It's a very famous site that shows the continuation of resistance in this place. If you were doing a timeline of protests, the Day of Mourning would be on that list. It's a completely nondescript site but incredibly important for us Blackfellas.' The building has been heritage-listed and is owned by the Metropolitan Local Aboriginal Land Council. The Day of Mourning, as well as forming the basis for protests held on 26 January to this day, also planted the seeds of NAIDOC Week, a celebration of First Nations culture and strength.

At the southern end of the CBD, Belmore Park is laid out like the garden of Central Station, a quiet green spot to kill time between trains. From time to time it has been full of the tents of homeless people, until the people are moved on, and early in the colony it was known as the Police Paddock, as it was next to the police barracks. It is as well a civic battleground, where the effects of Australian law on Aboriginal people have been strongly and continuously resisted. 'This is where I came to protests when I was a kid. We would be protesting against kids in custody, even back then, for land rights and Aboriginal rights, and against nuclear armament. I was brought here mostly by my dad. I just thought that was what you did on a Saturday.' In a direct lineage from the Day of Mourning, fifty years later the Bicentenary Protest march – thousands of Aboriginal protestors strong – arrived here to be greeted by a large contingent of non-Aboriginal supporters. The march then continued along Elizabeth Street, past the site of the original Day of Mourning, to Hyde Park, another site of resistance. Footage of the march shows the streets and parks thronging, and powerful speakers – Gary Foley, Linda Burney and others – making galvanising speeches on pride, survival and self-determination, while up at the harbour the arrival of the First Fleet was re-enacted.

'That challenging of the narrative of the bicentenary was probably shocking to many Australians who hadn't really thought about it. It certainly changed the conversation for First Nations people. You can go back to that point in time and identify when a large challenge to the national narrative started to take place. As I walk through here on my way to work, whether I'm going to the ABC or UTS, I remember those politics: the politics of self-determination, the politics of community control, the politics of sovereignty. That was very much a part of my developing world view.'

The protest tradition of this park, ideally located to receive protestors from all over the city and state through the doors of Central Station, has retained its roots as the movement takes on global solidarity. In the days of Larissa's childhood, 'people would set up their microphone and get fifty to a hundred people there and think, "Wow, the tide's really turned." And then when they had the Black Lives Matter protests here, there were so many people it seemed surreal. There were placards that said, "Check your white supremacy" or "White privilege is the problem". That was a whole language we didn't have back in those days. We used to talk about land rights, but even now everyone shouts, "What do we want? Land rights. When do we want them? Now." I love that there's a part of it that's stayed very dogged.'

For Larissa, the protests of the 1980s and '90s were shaping the future, not just for her but for a community. 'If I look at my close Aboriginal girlfriends – first-in-family, university-educated, professional women – we all grew up doing that kind of protest. For our generation, you really were the children of the street marches. That childhood of street marching and protesting and the politics of Redfern, of self-determination, is a big part of our world view. It's an important part of who we are.'

Moving down Chalmers Street, past the station and the tram tracks, you reach busy Cleveland Street. Cross over and you're in Redfern. On the corner of the intersection is a brightly painted terrace, a youth hostel, huge palm trees escaping from the tiny courtyard of the terrace next door. Continuing along Chalmers you pass another protest site: the old NSW Department of Community Service (DoCS) building, now called Family and Community Services. 'We often protest here because they take our kids and don't give them back, or they place them with white families when they should be putting them with extended black families.'

And then across Redfern Street is Redfern Park: a beautiful park with wide green stretches and a variety of trees, including very tall palm trees, the public-housing towers beyond, a bottle tree in the playground. The playground itself contains exquisite metal sculptures – a seed pod to clamber over, a water-play park in the form of poppy stems – by Badtjala artist Fiona Foley, a founding member of the Boomalli Aboriginal Artists Co-operative.

Standing here, you would not know it – no plaque, no sign – but history is all around. 'I can't remember why I was in Redfern on that day in 1992, but I was here with some friends and everyone started saying, "The prime minister's coming, the prime minister." When you look around now you think, "Well, why wouldn't he? It's such a lovely place," but at that time taxi drivers wouldn't come here. We had the most politically toughened, hardline activists in this community, who didn't brook anything from anyone.' When the word went around that Paul Keating was coming, 'We came down to have a look at the two-headed snake. The stage was here, and I was all the way back because I was a nobody. I could hear a couple of the old guard from Redfern heckling, but they shut up after a while, which was no small feat.'

When you watch footage of that day, 10 December 1992, the Australian launch of the International Year for the World's Indigenous People, you see a relatively young Keating climb the very few steps to the stage. Sol Bellear, deputy chair of the Aboriginal and Torres Strait Islander Commission (ATSIC), is there to introduce him; Stan Grant is MCing. Dancer and musician Matthew Doyle plays the yidaki, or didgeridoo. Doyle has said in an interview about that day that while the Prime Minister was standing on the stage, he repeated the traditional song he was playing, thinking, 'I'm gonna make him wait.' Without direction to leave the stage, he decided to stay for the speech. 'I just stood back from the microphone and listened.'

Keating said that the 'first Australians' were 'the people to whom the most injustice has been done'. The righting of this injustice, he said, begins with an 'act of recognition':

> Recognition that it was we who did the dispossessing. We took the traditional lands and smashed the traditional way of life. We brought the diseases and the alcohol. We committed the murders. We took the children from their mothers. We practised discrimination and exclusion. It was our ignorance and our prejudice, and our failure to imagine that these things could be done to us.

Larissa felt the significance of what was happening, way back in the crowd. 'I'll never forget how it felt to hear the prime minister say, "We were the ones who committed the massacres, and we were the ones who took the children." I was just finishing university and had been through an education system that didn't teach a single thing about any of that history. My classmates had incredibly uninformed, racist views. It felt profound to hear those words. In my mind, I felt like I could hear a pin drop.'

Larissa has revisited footage of the speech, using it in her films, watching it over and over. 'I thought, "If he's saying that now, we're going to be able to move forward." I didn't anticipate how much everything would be wound back. I'm not diminishing Kevin Rudd's apology to the Stolen Generations – I often go back and have a look at that too. What really strikes me about that day is, if you look through the crowds, the emotion of the old people – I still gasp at it. But it's a different thing to do a curated event on the opening of parliament than coming down here to Redfern, where nobody tells anybody what to do, what they can and can't say. This always feels like a really special spot to me.'

Back on Redfern Street it's bright and busy, people milling about between the bars and cafes and shops, and the train station at the other end of the street. The high-rises of the city are close and yet still this feels like its own distinctive place with its own community, even though it has become gentrified: an artisanal bakery on the corner, a real estate agent walking fast, selling a house over the phone.

Several important organisations had and still have their home here in the main street of the suburb. On the left, heading towards Redfern Station, is the Aboriginal Medical Service (AMS), founded in 1971 around the corner on Regent Street. This and the Aboriginal Legal Service were the first organisations to be controlled by the Aboriginal community in Australia. As well as bringing free health care to a community previously reliant on GPs and hospitals, where they were asked for cash upfront and often experienced shocking racism, the AMS was a hub of community amid a strong push towards self-determination. 'It used to be the place where everyone would come. I went to lots of meetings with my dad. I'd hear all the argy-bargy – they were not for the faint hearted. There was a lot of cursing and swearing. Those community organisations weren't just significant in what they did in terms of service delivery, but in being the heart of the community. Everything that was coming up would get discussed there.' As in the street marches, the young ones were watching and learning. 'We learned that we are the ones who need to have control of our future.'

Larissa experienced the community as a place of care from strong women, and of fierce intellectual engagement. 'We thought deeply about the politics of change. There were strategies like setting up community-controlled organisations – lunch and breakfast programs in the school. People read the political materials of the Black Panthers. Every Aboriginal man read *The Autobiography of Malcolm X*.' Amid this environment, Larissa's family shaped her outlook. Her father, Paul Behrendt, was an early archivist of the oral histories of Aboriginal people and a pioneer in academic Aboriginal studies. He had lived the injustices of the colony in his personal life – placed in an orphanage when his mother died, only reunited with his people much later in life – and used his experience with records to reunite other families via the Link-Up (NSW) Aboriginal Corporation. Larissa has said in interview that her mother, a white woman, 'has a great heart and social conscience. But it came at a cost to her, because she couldn't feel part of it herself. So she dropped us off at rallies and stayed outside.' Another influence was Paul's partner in the mid-1990s, author and activist Roberta Sykes, who encouraged Larissa to go to Harvard, her own alma mater, to continue her studies in law.

At the end of Redfern Street you enter the bustle and shadow around the station; above are the old TNT towers and the Watertower apartment block. Roberta lived in one of the apartments. 'She had one of those top balconies. She used to say she had a penthouse. She would sit with her cigarettes and her long nails with this view of what was happening in Redfern. She had a bird's eye view.' Another kind of surveillance, less friendly, was happening at the same time from the TNT towers, the tallest buildings in the area. 'There used to be police surveillance from them. They could see all the way down into the community.'

Across the street from the station, you can sit on a wall amid the immaculate landscaping of the Pemulwuy Project, a tower containing Aboriginal housing, student flats, a gym and a childcare centre, owned by the Aboriginal Housing Company. This is the site of the Block, the demolished cluster of terraces around Eveleigh Street, 'a site of great resistance and protest and still the heart of the community here, though it's changed so much'. There is still a row of the old terraces on Caroline Street, facing the green public space of Redfern Community Centre. Wrapped around a lone terrace on the corner of the green is *Welcome to Redfern*, the first artwork of the Eora Journey, created by Kamilaroi artist Reko Rennie with young local artists. The building is emblazoned with red, yellow and black stripes, and the words 'The BLOCK' on one side; on another, an Aboriginal man rows a bark canoe. 'You can see over here with these houses that this is what the whole place looked like. When I come down here later in the day, especially winter when it gets dark early, I can hear my dad because if I'd have said I was going to be on the Block after dark, he would have been really angry.'

Sitting under the tower of the Pemulwuy Project, we are somewhere between the old Redfern and the new. Amid the surviving terraces, and in the shadow of the new tower, the Redfern Community Centre fulfils some of the community functions the AMS did back in Larissa's younger days. 'People come to talk about protests or to mourn when someone's passed, or to celebrate, to raise awareness. It's a great space – you can put a microphone up and all of a sudden you've got a protest.' It's close to other services like the current AMS, and Mudgin-Gal Women's Place is at the other end of Caroline Street on Abercrombie. But the Block does feel very different now to Larissa. 'The place was about that self-determination, community-controlled organisations, the fierce politics of resistance. And I don't know that we've captured that yet – what was truly remarkable about this place.'

Within people, though, that past and its potential live on vividly. 'One of my favourite memories from around here is going into one of those old terrace houses. None were kept in good shape. Koori Radio used to be here and it had floorboards missing, but it was a community place. I was with my dad, visiting one of his friends here, an Aboriginal fella and lawyer – he was must have been one of the first. I remember walking into the little tenement house. There was a woman at the back doing the dishes. I must have been about eleven then. I thought she was the most beautiful woman I'd ever seen – not in a picture book, not anywhere. She was an Aboriginal woman and she was the most beautiful, elegant person. It was Linda Burney. When I was growing up, all the magazines had white people in them, everyone on TV was white, and she was just this objectively beautiful woman. She still is. I always associate her with here, because even though she went on to become a Member of Parliament, she was shaped by this place as much as I was.' Down at the terraces, a woman calls a young person inside, at exasperated length. It sounds like he might be in big trouble. 'I love this place,' Larissa says.

The final part of the walk takes us north along Abercrombie Street. The Redfern section is quiet, terrace balconies overhanging the street, people chatting on the road in the shade of eucalypts. Once you cross back over Cleveland Street, it's a major thoroughfare, with traffic heading up to Broadway, the city and the Bridge. Moving north, the perforated steel of the new UTS building comes into view. UTS is Larissa's destination, her workplace, specifically the Jumbunna Institute for Indigenous Education and Research, where she has felt 'able to shape a research unit that reflected what my community would have wanted me to do. Being so close to this community, they call us to account if they don't like something we're doing. I'll have to come down and front them.'

On this last stretch, tracing the thread between Larissa's upbringing at the fierce meetings of her childhood and her work now in academia, arts and the law, we pass a corner building that housed the Boomalli gallery in the 1990s. 'The old socialist bookshop was right next to it. I used to love going in and buying pamphlets and those little books stapled together – I'd take them home and underline them.' At Boomalli, 'Hetti Perkins and Brenda Croft were the first two curators, they were a few years older than me – they were hugely glamorous. It was such an amazing time. Bangarra Dance had started, and Stephen Page and his brothers came down from Brisbane and made it their own. A lot of those of us who were of that era got really involved in the arts, and so there was a renaissance around that time. That's the other memory for me of this place: it being where these unstoppable forces were rising: "Galleries aren't showing our art. Let's make our own. We're not seeing ourselves on the stage, let's set up our own. Our dance is not being danced."'

Boomalli and Bangarra, like many other community organisations, are still going strong: a legacy of those days. In Larissa's films and books, she celebrates the inventiveness of Aboriginal culture, its resilience and richness. Most recently, her series *The First Inventors* illustrates the astonishing record of culture and technology of Australia's first peoples. It explains too how specific knowledge of the world is contained in the stories handed down over hundreds of generations. In these stories, for example, the memory survives of lower sea levels all around Australia; it is a connection to people who lived in places that are now covered by ocean, transmitted through a record of knowledge that retains the presence of lived experience.

Larissa sends me on to visit a place where this connection feels alive to her, with a story to take with me. 'To be part of the world's oldest living culture is miraculous. When you think what we've survived over the last two hundred plus years, in this place of the colony, aggressive colonisation, the infestation of smallpox, the massacres, it's an extraordinary thing. Those places are still here, and that feeling is still there, and that history is still there. We're still here.'

AFTERWORD –
THE CITY IS ALIVE

Accompanied by Larissa's story, I walk on, across Broadway, behind UTS, following industrial history down to the water. Walking the Goods Line – the new path on the old elevated rail track – down to Darling Harbour, I pass the back of the Powerhouse Museum, whose building, red and saw-toothed, once provided electricity for trams. At Darling Harbour, the gleaming new entertainment and convention venues suggest we are living in some shiny clean future – no need to think about where we come from. But all through this area the waterways, Larissa told me, crept into the land. Further to the west in Glebe were kangaroo-hunting grounds where the men hunted, but at the harbour was where the women fished. Over at Cockle Bay Wharf was a 'strong women's place', containing their birthing site. Here on the western side, where the Australian National Maritime Museum stands, was a fishing place. Through the tangle of a tall ship's rigging are the apartment and office blocks of the city and the shining gold turret of Sydney Tower, but from here the women rowed out in bark canoes – nawi – with their fishing lines of cabbage tree and flax, animal fur and grass, their beautiful crescent fishhooks (burra) around their necks. This part of the city, Larissa said, 'still feels like it's a women's place, in spite of all the buildings and casinos and bridges. I feel like that that part of it's still there.'

A powerful woman carrying the old ways into the early days of the British colony was Cammeraygal woman Barangaroo, for whom the new development on the far shore is named. She was a resistant figure; on one occasion she and her husband Bennelong were invited to visit Governor Phillip, but she refused to go with him, breaking Bennelong's fishing spear in anger. She also refused to wear clothes, and attempted to intervene in the flogging of a convict. Barangaroo was outraged, particularly, by a profligate gift made by the colonists to the Cammeraygal people of 4000 fish, a wasteful violation that bypassed the role of women as fishers and providers. In 2018, Wiradjuri artist Emily McDaniel, along with four Indigenous artists, created an installation at Nawi Cove at Barangaroo in a spirit of restoration. There people were invited to pour harbour water into fish-shaped moulds to make ice sculptures. At sunset, the ice fish were taken by canoe and melted into the water, returned to the place from which they had been taken.

Gliding across to Barangaroo on the ferry, where the high-rises give way to colonial stores, to sandstone and headland, I think about the gift of story, the way it makes the city breathe. Sydney is alive in every corner with all that has happened here; all that has been remembered, dreamed and imagined. As we move through this place, we carry its lives with us, walking amid the layers of our collective spirit and imagining into the long, unfolding story to come.

NOTES

EPIGRAPHS

ix   'There are many versions of Sydney ...': Vanessa Berry, *Mirror Sydney: An Atlas of Reflections*, Giramondo, 2017, 4

ix   'Parisian writers always gave the street address ...': Rebecca Solnit, *Wanderlust: A History of Walking*, Granta, 2014 (2001), 210

INTRODUCTION – READING SYDNEY

3   '"as a kind of organization ..."': Rebecca Solnit, *Wanderlust: A History of Walking*, Granta, 2014 (2001), 197

3   '"In a dérive one or more persons ..."': Guy Debord, 'Theory of the dérive and definitions' (1958), *The People, Place, and Space Reader*, Routledge, 2014, 65–70

4   '... the city as a site of mystery ..."': Merlin Coverley, *Psychogeography*, Pocket Essentials, 2010, 13

6   '... what is "overlooked and odd" in "the hidden and enigmatic places"': Vanessa Berry, *Mirror Sydney: An Atlas of Reflections*, Giramondo, 2017, 3

10   'There was a sci-fi film shot in Sydney ...': Alex Proyas (director/co-writer), *Dark City*, feature film, New Line Cinema, 1998

11   '... the city is "a collection of stories ..."': Solnit, *Wanderlust*, 213

YINDYAMARRA – EVELEIGH AND CARRIAGEWORKS WITH JAZZ MONEY

15   'this city / thudded / over site sacred ...': Jazz Money, 'if that ghost is still here come morning', in *Mark the Dawn*, UQP, 2024, 37

16   '... "but tide rushing in ..."': Jazz Money, 'these are not spill marks but tide rushing in', in *Mark the Dawn*, 7

18   'pour upon the soft ground ...': Jazz Money, '100000', 2021, www.jazz.money/100000

19   'Efficiency drives, mass sackings and unpaid shifts ...': Eveleigh Stories, 'Strikes, unions and activism', nd, https://eveleighstories.com.au/stories/working-life/strikes-unions-and-activism

20   'Charles Madden, a Gadigal Elder and artist ...': Art Gallery of NSW, 'Thea Anamara Perkins: Poppy Chicka', 2020, www.artgallery.nsw.gov.au/prizes/archibald/2020/30238/

HISTORY BENEATH YOUR FEET – SURRY HILLS WITH FIONA KELLY McGREGOR

29	'Clisdell Street, Maisie had said ...': Fiona Kelly McGregor, *Iris*, Picador, 2022, 186
30	'"She drew me in through sheer force of personality ..."': Fiona Kelly McGregor, 'Surro', *Buried Not Dead*, Giramondo, 2021, 259
31	'"All along the gangplank men held signs ..."': McGregor, *Iris*, 8
31–32	'"You are walking towards Clisdell Street ..."': McGregor, 'Surro', 244
33	'"The old red brick flats are light ..."': McGregor, 'Surro', 246
33	'He ran up to Belvoir Street ...': McGregor, *Iris*, 306
35	'... an exhibition of queer history ...': Miles Pattenden and Michael Barbezat, 'Remembering Fabian LoSchiavo: Australian nun, social activist, religious leader', *ABC Religion & Ethics*, 22 May 2023, www.abc.net.au/religion/fabian-loschiavo-australian-nun-religious-leader/102377046
36	'Iris haunted me ...': Fiona Kelly McGregor, The life and times of Iris Webber, marginal crim of sly-grog Sydney, PhD thesis, University of Technology Sydney, 2017, http://opus.lib.uts.edu.au/handle/10453/123265
39	'Members of the collective worked ...': Lenny Anne Low, 'Imperial Slacks: "They f---ed, made art, drank, slept and contributed to the city"', *Sydney Morning Herald*, 7 August 2015, www.smh.com.au/entertainment/art-and-design/imperial-slacks-they-fed-made-art-drank-slept-and-contributed-to-the-city-20150805-giqb5f.html
39	'Ada went by various names ...': Fiona is credited as the first to make this connection: Bren Donnellan, 'Becoming known: The quest for Black Ada', information sheet, Qtopia Sydney, 2024
39	'... "a sprinkling of 'know-all-girls' ..."': The reference to 'know-all-girls' is from oral testimony first published in *Campaign* magazine and reproduced in Garry Wotherspoon, *City of the Plain: History of a Gay Sub-culture*, Hale & Iremonger, 1991
39	'it seemed the most natural thing ...': McGregor, *Iris*, 185

VERTICALS OF LIGHT – THE ROCKS, WALSH BAY AND CIRCULAR QUAY WITH GAIL JONES

45	'There was confusion at first ...': Gail Jones, *Five Bells*, Vintage, 2011, 1
45	'Ellie, a new arrival ...': Jones, *Five Bells*, 4
46	'The first Australian Cubist landscape ...': 'About: The Bridge, Dorrit Black', Art Gallery of South Australia, https://www.agsa.sa.gov.au/collection-publications/collection/works/the-bridge/24065/#about-narrative-2098
47	'Gail's novel *One Another* ...': Gail Jones, *One Another*, Text Publishing, 2024

47	'He wrote of Sydney Harbour ...': Joseph Conrad, *The Mirror of the Sea*, John Grant, 1925 (1906), 121
48	'Crowds of men and women ...': Walt Whitman, 'Crossing Brooklyn Ferry', in *Leaves of Grass*, Thayer and Eldridge, 1856, www.poetryfoundation.org/poems/45470/crossing-brooklyn-ferry
49	'... "wander the city, finding the pleasure ..."': Jones, *Five Bells*, 21
50	'*Rats* was another memento ...': Damian Holmes, 'HASSELL lights the way to Walsh Bay for Vivid Sydney', *World Landscape Architecture*, 7 June 2013, https://worldlandscapearchitect.com/hassell-lights-the-way-to-walsh-bay-for-vivid-sydney/
52	'... "We are no longer quite ourselves ..."': Virginia Woolf, 'Street haunting', in *The Death of the Moth and Other Essays*, Hogarth Press, 1942, 23
52	'... "the shell-like covering" ...': Woolf, 'Street haunting', 20
52	'"Into each of these lives ..."': Woolf, 'Street haunting', 28
55	'"Roland Barthes talks about ..."': Roland Barthes, 'Leaving the movie theater', in Phillip Lopate (ed), *The Art of the Personal Essay*, Anchor Books, 1995; Italo Calvino, *Road to San Giovanni*, Jonathan Cape, 1993
55	'"That blue luminescence ..."': John Olsen, 'The inside story of Olsen's celebrated Opera House mural', Sydney Opera House, 24 May 2023, www.sydneyoperahouse.com/our-story/art-at-the-house/john-olsen-sydney-opera-house-inside-story-olsens-celebrated-opera-house-mural

PARRAMATTA WILL NEVER BE COMPLETE – PARRAMATTA WITH EDA GUNAYDIN

61	'All along the river ...': Eda Gunaydin, 'Second city', in *Root & Branch: Essays on inheritance*, NewSouth, 2022, 32
62	'I am loath to think ...': Eda Gunaydin, 'Western medicine', in *Root & Branch*, NewSouth, 2022, 154
63	'... "Paramatta has often felt ..."': Gunaydin, 'Second city', 38
63	'... "sustained smiling"': Gunaydin, 'Second city', 28
63	'I wrote some of these mundane details ...': Gunaydin, 'Second city', 29
65	'In Eda's essay ...': Eda Gunaydin, 'Street as studio', in Cherine Fahd, *Being Together: Parramatta Yearbook*, Museum of Contemporary Art Australia, 2022, 8–9, www.mca.com.au/c3west/cherine-fahd-parramatta-yearbook/
66	'In a news article about the new school building ...': Jordan Baker, 'Classrooms with a view: Inside Sydney's new $225 million high school', *Sydney Morning Herald*, 24 July 2019, www.smh.com.au/education/classrooms-with-a-view-inside-sydney-s-new-225-million-high-school-20190723-p529zy.html

67	'In Rebecca Solnit's writing ...': Rebecca Solnit, 'Paris, or botanizing on the asphalt', in *Wanderlust: A History of Walking*, Granta, 2014 (2001), 204–205
67	'there were young people of colour ...': Gunaydin, 'Second city', 30–31
68	'"I should have known this ..."': Gunaydin, 'Second city', 36
70	'"Country bears the scars of its people ..."': Willem Brussen, 'The tree still grows the river still flows: Country listens, Country remembers', *The River Series*, Powerhouse Museum, https://powerhouse.com.au/stories/the-tree-still-grows#the-tree-still-grows-the-river-still-flows-country-listens-country-remembers
71	'Part of Eda's work ...': 'Parracons Poetry Trail', WestWords, nd, www.westwords.com.au/project/parracons/
71	'stopped in the middle of Parramatta Park ...': Gunaydin, 'Second city', 40–41
73	'In 2017 they gained a national heritage listing ...': International Coalition of Sites of Conscience, 'Parramatta Female Factory Precinct Project – Australia', 2025, www.sitesofconscience.org/membership/parramatta-female-factory-precinct-project-australia/

SLIPPING INTO THE CURRENT – KING STREET, NEWTOWN WITH VANESSA BERRY

77	'I first visited King Street ...': Vanessa Berry, 'Newtown in the 1990s map', blog post, *Mirror Sydney*, 21 October 2013, https://mirrorsydney.wordpress.com/2013/10/21/newtown-in-the-1990s-map/
77–78	'Her memoir *Ninety9* ...': Vanessa Berry, *Ninety9*, Giramondo, 2013
78	'In Vanessa's *Mirror Sydney* blog ...': Berry, 'Newtown in the 1990s map'
79	'Bob Gould, early opponent of the Vietnam War ...': Steph Harmon, 'Gould's Book Arcade: The political, literary legacy of Newtown's dusty wonder', *The Guardian*, 27 November 2017, www.theguardian.com/books/2017/nov/27/goulds-book-arcade-the-political-literary-legacy-of-newtowns-dusty-wonder
80–81	'In her essay "The Writer's Clutter" ...': Vanessa Berry, 'The writer's clutter', *Sydney Review of Books*, 1 December 2019, https://sydneyreviewofbooks.com/essays/the-writers-clutter
83	'Pryor said of the painting ...': Barry Divola, 'King(s) Street', *Sydney Morning Herald*, 25 August 2011, www.smh.com.au/entertainment/art-and-design/kings-street-20110825-1jbi4.html
83–84	'Vanessa writes of her evening walks ...': Berry, 'The writer's clutter'
86	'In that essay Vanessa writes ...': Vanessa Berry, 'Memorial stores', in *Mirror Sydney: An Atlas of Reflections*, Giramondo, 2017, 157

87   'As Vanessa writes in her essay "Excavating St Peters" ...': Vanessa Berry, 'Excavating St Peters', in *Mirror Sydney*, 141

THE IDEA OF A BEACH – FRESHWATER WITH MALCOLM KNOX

93   'A claw of sandstone clasps its jewels ...': Malcolm Knox, *Bluebird*, Allen & Unwin, 2020, 15

94   'In *Bluebird*, the derelict protagonist ...': Knox, *Bluebird*, 16

95   'From 1923, for eighty-five years ...': John Morcombe, 'How campers at Freshwater led to the suburb's name being changed to Harbord', *Manly Daily*, 14 July 2020, https://freshie.org.au/2021/02/09/how-campers-at-freshwater-led-to-the-suburbs-name-being-changed-to-harbord/

96   'In Malcolm's novel *The Life* ...': Malcolm Knox, *The Life*, Allen & Unwin, 2012, 63

TODAY – YAGOONA AND BANKSTOWN WITH SHEILA NGỌC PHẠM

105   'Whenever I have touched on Western Sydney's history ...': Sheila Ngọc Phạm, 'Western Sydney is dead, long live Western Sydney!', *Sydney Review of Books*, 13 June 2022, https://sydneyreviewofbooks.com/essays/western-sydney-is-dead-long-live-western-sydney

106   'Sheila's autobiographical essay ...': Sheila Ngọc Phạm, 'An elite education', *Sydney Review of Books*, 12 June 1019, https://sydneyreviewofbooks.com/essay/an-elite-education-sheila-ngoc-pham/

107   '... the name Yagoona means *today*, or *now* ...': Jakelin Troy, *The Sydney Language*, Aboriginal Studies Press, 2021 (1994), 80

108   'In an article about the pressures ...': Sheila Ngọc Phạm, 'Sydney lockdown: If we're all in this together, let's ditch the scapegoating', *The Guardian*, 27 July 2021, www.theguardian.com/commentisfree/2021/jul/27/sydney-lockdown-if-were-all-in-this-together-lets-ditch-the-scapegoating

109   'The rector is fighting ...': Andrew Taylor, 'Anglican Diocese fights heritage orders that prevent church redevelopment', *Sydney Morning Herald*, 2 July 2023, www.smh.com.au/national/nsw/anglican-diocese-fights-heritage-orders-that-prevent-church-redevelopment-20230622-p5dip2.html

110   'A tree-cover map of Sydney ...': Jan Orton and Sophie Moore, 'Tree canopy in Greater Sydney, how are we doing?', *The Fifth Estate*, 14 February 2024, https://thefifthestate.com.au/columns/spinifex/tree-canopy-in-greater-sydney-how-are-we-doing/

111   'Sheila references commentary ...': George Megalogenis 'In Conversation: Underwog: Migrant integration and influence in postwar Australia', *Griffith Review*, no 69, 2020, 286–291

111	'Sheila examines the complexities of diasporic belonging ...': Sheila Ngọc Phạm, 'Flags of my father: The question of national identity', *Kill Your Darlings*, 7 January 2013, www.killyourdarlings.com.au/article/flags-of-my-father/
111	'"I didn't understand ..."': Pham, 'Flags of my father'
112	'... "My name is Bryan Brown ..."': National Press Club of Australia, 'In full: Bryan Brown AM addresses the National Press Club of Australia', video, YouTube, 20 July 2023, www.youtube.com/watch?v=U4jn0wgKi0g
112	'Now in the libraries ...': Sheila Ngọc Phạm, 'A love letter to libraries', *Eureka Street*, 10 August 2018, www.eurekastreet.com.au/article/a-love-letter-to-libraries
115	'You can see these treasures online ...': Myling Nguyen (@mylyn_eat_zombie), '350 Chapel Road Bankstown', Instagram post, 1 October 2022, www.instagram.com/p/CjKHr-WDEwB/; 'A tiny paper dog', Instagram post, 4 September 2023, www.instagram.com/p/CwvDtTYhw4G/
116	'Both recall hearing stories ...': Andy Butler, 'Drum majors: James Nguyen & Victoria Pham on RE:SOUNDING', Diasporic Vietnamese Artists Network, 3 March 2021, https://dvan.org/2021/03/drum-majors-james-nguyen-victoria-pham/
117	'Writing about the baths ...': Bryan Brown, 'Bryan Brown's Bankstown baths: "I learned swimming, but also about friendship and loyalty"', *The Guardian*, 10 November 2019, www.theguardian.com/lifeandstyle/2019/nov/08/bryan-browns-bankstown-baths-i-learned-swimming-but-also-about-friendship-and-loyalty
118	'It bothered her ...': Sheila Ngọc Phạm, 'Food neighbourhoods #44: Cabramatta', *The Menu*, 18 July 2023, https://monocle.com/radio/shows/the-menu/food-neighbourhoods-344/
119	'... one of Bankstown's humble but inviting cafes ...': Sheila Ngọc Phạm, 'The late-night meal in Ho Chi Minh City that inspired a Bankstown café's key dish', *SBS Food*, 10 July 2020, www.sbs.com.au/food/article/the-late-night-meal-in-ho-chi-minh-city-that-inspired-a-bankstown-cafes-key-dish/mgdez5sen
119	'... Sheila quotes a phrase ...': Vanessa Berry, *Mirror Sydney: An Atlas of Reflections*, Giramondo, 2017, 210

TIDAL CITY – RUSHCUTTERS BAY PARK AND ELIZABETH BAY WITH DELIA FALCONER

123	'Like Los Angeles ...': Delia Falconer, *Sydney*, NewSouth, 2020 (2010), 3
124	'Speaking on ABC Radio National ...': Jonathan Green (host) and Delia Falconer, 'Lost and found – sandstone', radio episode,

Blueprint for Living, ABC Radio National, 19 October 2019, www.abc.net.au/listen/programs/blueprintforliving/lostandfound-sandstone/11615898

125 'Denis Byrne, a geographer, talks about Sydney ...': Denis Byrne, 'Remembering the Elizabeth Bay reclamation and the Holocene sunset in Sydney Harbour', *Environmental Humanities*, vol 9, no 1, 2017, 40–59

126 'Talking about sandstone ...': Green and Falconer, 'Lost and found – sandstone'

127 'Delia mentions Helen Garner's essay ...': Helen Garner, 'Water notes', *HEAT*, no. 10, 2005, 27–34

127–28 'Twenty thousand years ago, as Grace Karskens writes ...': Grace Karskens, *The Colony*, Allen & Unwin, 2009, 29–30

128 'Ian Hoskins, in his history of the harbour ...': Ian Hoskins, *Sydney Harbour: A history*, NewSouth, 2022 (2009), 3

128–29 'A large river red gum ...': Paul Irish, 'Barcom Glen', Barani: Sydney's Aboriginal History, 2013, www.sydneybarani.com.au/sites/barcom-glen/

129 'Kate Grenville's fictional version of Bea ...': Kate Grenville, *Lilian's Story*, Text Publishing, 2021 (1985), 303

129 '... literary sites begin to gather ...': Jill Dimond and Peter Kirkpatrick, *Literary Sydney: A Walking Guide*, UQP, 2000, 102

130–31 'Linda Jaivin, wrote in 2005 ...': Linda Jaivin, 'From BoHo to PoHo', *The Monthly*, July 2005, 38–43

131 '"... 'windrowing', as poet Les Murray puts it ..."': Les Murray, 'The Flying-Fox Dreaming, Wingham Brush, New South Wales', in *Ethnic Radion*, Angus & Robertson, 1977

131–32 '"I always think of playwright and novelist ..."': Sumner Locke Elliott, *Fairyland: A Novel*, Harper & Row, 1990

132 'Later, in the 1820s ...': 'Elizabeth Town', Barani: Sydney's Aboriginal History, www.sydneybarani.com.au/sites/elizabeth-town/

133 'I seem to remember ...': Delia Falconer, 'The intimacy of the table', *Review of Contemporary Fiction*, vol 27, no 3, 2007, 56–64

134 '... "a 'crooked, intimate, compact' town ..."': Karskens, *The Colony*, 2

134 'Even this grand building, though ...': 'King's Cross: Bohemian life in Sydney', Museums of History New South Wales, 2022, https://mhnsw.au/stories/general/kings-cross-bohemian-life-sydney/

134 'In her essay "A city of one's own" ...': Delia Falconer, 'A City of One's Own: Women's Sydney', *Dictionary of Sydney*, 2014, https://dictionaryofsydney.org/entry/a_city_of_ones_own_womens_sydney

134	'... she references the character Nora Porteous ...': Jessica Anderson, *Tirra Lirra by the River*, Penguin, 1978
135	'"It is Sydney's wild mix ..."': Falconer, *Sydney*, 170

WALKING ON CAMMERAYGAL COUNTRY – NORTH WILLOUGHBY AND MIDDLE COVE WITH JAKELIN TROY

139	'I am a member of the Ngyamitjimitung clan ...': Jakelin Troy, 'Standing on the ground and writing on the sky: An Indigenous exploration of place, time, and histories', in Ann McGrath, Laura Rademaker and Jakelin Troy (eds), *Everywhen: Australia and the Language of Deep History*, University of Nebraska Press, 2023, 57
139	'In the 1980s and 1990s ...' Jakelin Troy, *The Sydney Language*, Aboriginal Studies Press, 2021 (1994)
144	'... she describes in her essay ...': Jakelin Troy, 'Walking, sketching and dogs: Autoethnography in the time of fire and rona', in *Earth Cries: A Climate Change Anthology*, Sydney University Press, 2021
147	'In a book called *Everywhen* ...': Troy, 'Standing on the ground and writing on the sky', 37–56
148	'"When I spoke my language for the first time ..."': Troy, 'Standing on the ground and writing on the sky', 66

SOME SECRET TO LIFE – CASULA AND LIVERPOOL WITH MAX EASTON

153	'Helen remembered ...': Max Easton, *The Magpie Wing*, Giramondo, 2021, 182
153	'... *Paradise Estate* ...': Max Easton, *Paradise Estate*, Giramondo, 2023
154	'... "early forays into punk music ..."': Easton, *The Magpie Wing*, 68
155–56	'... "none of the ideas kicked around ..."': Max Easton, 'Can the Magpie speak?', *Sydney Review of Books*, 27 October 2021, https://sydneyreviewofbooks.com/essay/easton-can-the-magpie-speak/
157	'When he left for work ...': Easton, *The Magpie Wing*, 29
159	'Here Max's character Walt ...': Easton, *The Magpie Wing*, 213
159–60	'Walt flirts with and provokes ...': Easton, *The Magpie Wing*, 115
161	'Max describes in a piece for the State Library ...': Max Easton, 'Max Easton's self portrait', *Openbook*, Autumn 2024, www.sl.nsw.gov.au/stories/max-eastons-self-portrait

A MAGIC TO THE MIRE – KINGS CROSS, DARLINGHURST AND SURRY HILLS WITH NEAL DRINNAN

167	'The street's glamour is its people ...': Neal Drinnan, *Glove Puppet*, Penguin, 1998, 53
169–70	'The Gazebo bar has a brief but significant cameo ...': Neal Drinnan, *Quill: A Novel*, Penguin, 2000, 54–55

171	'Gary Wotherspoon writes ...': Gary Wotherspoon, 'Darlinghurst and me', in Anna Clark, Gabrielle Kemmis and Tamson Pietsch (eds), *My Darlinghurst*, NewSouth, 2023, 241
172	'For two years in a row ...': Trish Luker and Neal Drinnan (eds), *Fruit Salad: A Compote of Contemporary Gay & Lesbian Writing*, Sydney Gay & Lesbian Mardi Gras Ltd, 1997; Neal Drinnan and Trish Luker (eds), *20 & Lit: A Free Taste of Lesbian & Gay Fiction, Faction, Farce and Friction*, Sydney Gay & Lesbian Mardi Gras Ltd, 1998
174	'... "... I wrote a novel set in New Zealand ..."': Graeme Aitken, *50 Ways of Saying Fabulous*, Random House, 1995
174–75	'... "We sold well over 2000 copies ..."': Timothy Conigrave, *Holding the Man*, McPhee Gribble, 1995; Graeme Aitken, *Vanity Fierce*, Vintage, 1998; Paul Freeman, *Ian Roberts: Finding Out*, Random House, 1997
175	'... a tunnel that supplied water from the Lachlan Swamps ...': Michael Koziol, 'Secret Sydney tunnel halts construction of boutique hotel', *Sydney Morning Herald*, 21 May 2023, www.smh.com.au/national/nsw/secret-sydney-tunnel-halts-construction-of-boutique-hotel-20230530-p5dcdw.html
175–76	'In *Quill*, Blaise dramatises the famous Sydney hailstorm ...': Drinnan, *Quill*, 112
176–77	'Surry Hills is reimagined as "the Gilgal"...': Neal Drinnan, *Izzy and Eve*, Green Candy, 2006, 5–6

FEEL EACH PART OF YOUR FOOT ON THE GROUND – BRONTE AND CLOVELLY WITH BETH YAHP

181	'We eat our eggs and toast ...': Beth Yahp, *Eat First, Talk Later*, Vintage, 2015, 94–95
183	'The healing properties of green places ...': Drusilla Modjeska, 'The informed imagination', *Meanjin*, vol 74, no 2, 2015, https://meanjin.com.au/memoir/the-informed-imagination/
185	'... the task is to "try to give equal attention ..."': Beth Yahp and Show Ying Xin, '"I'm a hyphenated writer": An interview with Beth Yahp', *Southeast Asian Review of English*, vol 57, no 1, 2020, https://sare.um.edu.my/index.php/SARE/article/view/25295/11978
186	'... for what the French writer Georges Perec called the "infraordinary" ...': Georges Perec, 'Approaches to what?', *Cause Commune*, no. 5, February 1973, quoted in Beth Yahp, 'Small pleasures: Tracings of the endotic in everyday spaces, acts and bodies', *Life Writing*, vol 17, no 4, 2020, 581–589
187–88	'... "Later, at home, squatting hunched ..."': Yahp, *Eat First, Talk Later*, 315

CREATING A LIBRARY – BANKSTOWN AND PUNCHBOWL BOYS' HIGH SCHOOL WITH MICHAEL MOHAMMED AHMAD

195 'I will take your weightless body ...': Michael Mohammed Ahmad, *The Other Half of You*, Hachette, 2021, 240

196 'Mohammed talks about the seminal work ...': Ghassan Hage, *White Nation: Fantasies of White Supremacy in a Multicultural Society*, Routledge, 1998

198 'The Muslim male, he says, was a kind of folk devil.': George Morgan and Scott Poynting, 'Introduction: The transnational folk devil', in George Morgan and Scott Poynting (eds), *Global Islamophobia: Muslims and Moral Panic in the West*, Ashgate Publishing, 2012, 15–28

202 '"We cannot talk about freedom ..."': Sweatshop, www.sweatshop.ws; the original bell hooks quote appeared in Sut Jhally (director), *bell hooks: Cultural Criticism and Transformation*, documentary, 1997, transcript by Media Education Foundation, 2005, www.mediaed.org/transcripts/Bell-Hooks-Transcript.pdf

203 '"The school building was surrounded ..."': Michael Mohammed Ahmad, '"Eye for eye, tooth for tooth": 9/11 inside Punchbowl Boys' High', *Sydney Morning Herald*, 3 September 2021, www.smh.com.au/culture/books/eye-for-eye-tooth-for-tooth-9-11-inside-punchbowl-boys-high-20210819-p58k2x.html

203 '... a representation Mohammed explores ...': Michael Mohammed Ahmad, 'Lebs and Punchbowl Prison', *Sydney Review of Books*, 28 November 2016, https://sydneyreviewofbooks.com/essays/lebs-and-punchbowl-prison

204 '..."we are our fastest, we are most united ..."': Michael Mohammed Ahmad, *The Lebs*, Hachette, 2018, 48–9

204 'Not long ago ...': *Books that Made Us*, episode 1, 'People', directed by Sally Aitken, 2021

A PLACE OF REVELATIONS – COOKS RIVER WITH MICHELLE DE KRETSER

209 '... the park detached itself ...': Michelle de Kretser, *The Life to Come*, Allen & Unwin, 2017, 5–6

209 'On its shore the famed Bidjigal warrior Pemulwuy ...': Jordan Baker, Brook Mitchell and the Visual Stories Team, 'How Sydney's most toxic river is fighting back', *Sydney Morning Herald*, 19 June 2023, www.smh.com.au/interactive/2023/cooks-river/

210 'That spring, Frances walked along the river ...': Michelle de Kretser, *Springtime: A Ghost Story*, Allen & Unwin, 2014, 1

211 'In a piece about this loss ...': Michelle de Kretser, 'Missing Minnie: A dog's death leaves a crushing sense of loss', *Sydney Morning Herald*, 4 May 2018, www.smh.com.au/entertainment/missing-minnie-a-dogs-death-leaves-a-crushing-sense-of-loss-20180426-h0z98y.html

211 'For the narrator in Michelle's latest novel ...': Michelle de Kretser, *Theory & Practice*, Text, 2024, 75
213 '... "artist-inhabitants" ...': Jacqueline Larcombe, 'Columns and roses: Reading the surfaces of a neighbourhood', master's thesis, University of Sydney, 2021, https://ses.library.usyd.edu.au/handle/2123/28885
214 'In *Theory & Practice*, Michelle writes of ...': de Kretser, *Theory & Practice*, 128; *The Life to Come*, 345
215 'For Christabel, images of Sri Lanka ...': de Kretser, *The Life to Come*, 298
215 'The city smelled briny and fumy ...': de Kretser, *The Life to Come*, 29
215–16 'The Russian Sydneysider Joseph ...': de Kretser, *Springtime*, 28

ALWAYS HERE – CITY AND REDFERN WITH LARISSA BEHRENDT
221 'I remember my grandmother telling me ...': Larissa Behrendt, 'Under skin, in blood', *Overland*, no 203, 2011, overland.org.au/previous-issues/issue-203/fiction-larissa-behrendt/
223 'The work that Tony Albert and others ...': 'About', Boomalli, 2025, boomalli.com.au/about/
224 'Here amid the workaday bustle ...': Department of Climate Change, Energy, the Environment and Water, 'Cyprus Hellene Club - Australian Hall, 150-152 Elizabeth St, Sydney, NSW, Australia', Australian Heritage Database, n.d., www.environment.gov.au/cgi-bin/ahdb/search.pl?mode=place_detail;place_id=105937
225 WE, representing THE ABORIGINES ...': 'The 1938 Day of Mourning', AIATSIS, n.d., https://aiatsis.gov.au/explore/day-of-mourning
225 'The Day of Mourning, as well as forming ...': NITV Staff Writer, 'Timeline: From the beginning of NAIDOC Week until now', NITV, 6 November 2020, www.sbs.com.au/nitv/article/timeline-from-the-beginning-of-naidoc-week-until-now/bofw495od
225–26 'From time to time it has ...': 'History of Belmore Park', City of Sydney, 4 January 2018, www.cityofsydney.nsw.gov.au/histories-local-parks-playgrounds/history-belmore-park
226 '... fifty years later the Bicentenary Protest march ...': Emma Cupitt, 'Radio Redfern, 26 January 1988', *Aboriginal History*, no 45, 2021, 33–55, https://press-files.anu.edu.au/downloads/press/n9914/pdf/02_cupitt.pdf
228 'Sol Bellear, deputy chair ...': Sol Bellear, Stan Grant, Matthew Doyle, Larissa Behrendt, Lorena Allam and Amanda Meade, '"Keating told the truth": Stan Grant, Larissa Behrendt and others remember the Redfern speech 30 years on', *The Guardian*,

	10 December 2022, www.theguardian.com/australia-news/2022/dec/10/paul-keating-redfern-speech-30-year-anniverary
229	'Recognition that it was we who did the dispossessing ...': ABCLibrarySales, 'ABC News: Paul Keating Redfern Speech (1992)', video, YouTube, 10 December 1992, www.youtube.com/watch?v=Z6dnDkvdTXA
230	'As well as bringing free health care ...': 'Aboriginal Medical Service: Our history & future', Aboriginal Medical Service, 2021, https://amsredfern.org.au/our-history-future/
231	'He had lived the injustices of the colony ...': Larissa Behrendt and Jason Behrendt, 'Paul Arthur Behrendt (1939–2006)', *Australian Dictionary of Biography*, 2024, https://adb.anu.edu.au/biography/behrendt-paul-arthur-33661/text42123
231	'Another influence was Paul's partner ...': Malcolm Knox, 'Lunch with Larissa Behrendt', *Sydney Morning Herald*, 18 September 2010, www.smh.com.au/entertainment/celebrity/lunch-with-larissa-behrendt-20100917-15gbs.html
232	'Wrapped around a lone terrace ...': City of Sydney, 'Eora Journey: Recognition in the public domain', n.d., www.cityofsydney.nsw.gov.au/cultural-support-funding/eora-journey-recognition-public-domain
234	'Most recently, her series *The First Inventors* ...': Larissa Behrendt (director), *The First Inventors*, TV series, SBS, 2023

AFTERWORD – THE CITY IS ALIVE

237	'...the women rowed out in bark canoes ...': Grace Karskens, 'Barangaroo and the Eora Fisherwomen', *Dictionary of Sydney*, 2014, https://dictionaryofsydney.org/entry/barangaroo_and_the_eora_fisherwomen
237–38	'A powerful woman carrying the old ways ...': Grace Karskens, 'Barangaroo and the Eora Fisherwomen'
238	'In 2018, Wiradjuri artist Emily McDaniel ...': Luke Wong, 'Sydney Harbour artwork honours Aboriginal fisherwomen and the history of Barangaroo', *ABC News*, 10 January 2018, www.abc.net.au/news/2018-01-10/four-thousand-fish-ice-sculpture-artwork-sydney-barangaroo/9314048

ABOUT THE WALKERS

Michael Mohammed Ahmad is the founding director of Sweatshop Literacy Movement and the author of three award-winning novels: *The Tribe* (Giramondo, 2014), *The Lebs* (Hachette, 2018) and *The Other Half of You* (Hachette, 2021). He is also the editor of several critically acclaimed anthologies, including *After Australia* (Affirm Press, 2020). Mohammed received his Doctorate of Creative Arts from Western Sydney University in 2017.

Distinguished Professor Larissa Behrendt AO is a Euahleyai/Gamillaroi woman and Laureate Fellow at the Jumbunna Institute of Indigenous Education and Research at the University of Technology Sydney. Larissa's novels have won several awards including the David Unaipon Award and the Victorian Premier's Literary Award for Indigenous Writing. She is also an award-winning filmmaker and the host of *Speaking Out* on ABC Radio. Larissa was awarded an Order of Australia in 2020 for her work in Indigenous education, the law and the arts. In 2021, she received the Human Rights Medal from the Australian Human Rights Commission. Larissa is a Native Title holder and a member of the Yuwaalaraay Euahlayi Aboriginal Corporation RNTBC, as well as a member of the Metropolitan Local Aboriginal Land Council.

Vanessa Berry is a writer who lives and works on Gadigal land. In her writing she investigates relationships between autobiography, time, places and objects. She is the author of books including *Mirror Sydney*, *Calendar* and *Gentle and Fierce*, and the zine series *I am a Camera*. She is a Lecturer in Creative Writing at the University of Sydney.

Michelle de Kretser is a novelist who was born in Sri Lanka and lives on unceded Gadigal land in Warrane/Sydney. Her fiction has won several awards, and her most recent novel is *Theory & Practice*.

Neal Drinnan was born in Melbourne. He has worked in publishing and journalism for many years and ran an independent bookshop in regional Victoria for a decade. He is the author of six novels – *Glove Puppet*, *Pussy's Bow*, *Quill*, the Lambda award-winning *Izzy and Eve*, *Rare Bird of Truth* and *Rural Liberties* – as well as true crime *Devil's Grip* and a travel guide, *The Rough Guide to Gay and Lesbian Australia*.

Max Easton is a writer from Sydney. He is the creator of *Barely Human*, a zine and podcast series exploring underground music's ties to counterculture and subculture. He is the author of two novels published by Giramondo: *The Magpie Wing* (longlisted for the 2022 Miles Franklin Literary Award), and its follow-up *Paradise Estate*, released in 2023. He is currently working on his third novel.

Dr Delia Falconer is the author of two novels (*The Service of Clouds* and *The Lost Thoughts of Soldiers*) and two works of nonfiction (*Sydney* and *Signs and Wonders: Dispatches from a Time of Beauty and Loss*). Her books have been awarded and shortlisted nationally and internationally across the categories of fiction, nonfiction, innovation, biography, history and research. She is the Acting Head of Creative Writing at the University of Technology Sydney.

Eda Gunaydin is a Turkish-Australian essayist and researcher whose writing explores class, Western Sydney, intergenerational trauma and diaspora. She has been published widely in publications including *Meanjin*, *HEAT*, *Sydney Review of Books*, *Cordite* and others. Her debut essay collection *Root & Branch: Essays on inheritance* won the 2023 Victorian Premier's Literary Award for Non-Fiction, and was shortlisted for the 2023 Australian Book Industry Awards' Matt Richell Award for New Writer of the Year. She lives on Wangal land.

Gail Jones is a former academic, and the author of two short-story collections and eleven novels. Her work has been translated internationally and awarded several prizes in Australia. Originally from Western Australia, she now lives in Sydney.

Malcolm Knox grew up in Sydney. Since 1994 he has written for the *Sydney Morning Herald*, and has won three Walkley Awards and a Human Rights Award. His novels include *Summerland*; *A Private Man*, winner of a Ned Kelly Award; *Jamaica*, which won the Colin Roderick Award and was shortlisted in the 2008 Prime Minister's Literary Awards; *The Life*; *The Wonder Lover*; *Bluebird*; and *The First Friend*. His many nonfiction titles include *Boom: The Underground History of Australia*; *From Gold Rush to GFC*, which won the 2013 Ashurst Business Literature Prize; and *Bradman's War*, shortlisted in the 2013 Prime Minister's Literary Awards.

Fiona Kelly McGregor has published eight books, most recently the novel *Iris*, nominated for many awards including the Miles Franklin, a NSW Premier's Literary Award, the ALS Gold Medal and the Stella Prize. Her novel *Indelible Ink* won *The Age* Book of the Year and was published in French by Actes

Sud. McGregor's nonfiction includes essay collection *Buried Not Dead*, shortlisted for a Victorian Premier's Literary Award for Non-Fiction; genre-busting photo essay *A Novel Idea*; and travel memoir *Strange Museums*. McGregor writes for the *Saturday Paper*, *Sydney Review of Books*, *Art Link*, *Art Monthly* and more, and will publish *The Trap*, a follow-up to *Iris*, in early 2026.

Jazz Money is a Wiradjuri poet and artist producing works that encompass installation, digital, performance, film and print. Their writing and art has been presented, performed and published nationally and internationally. Jazz's debut poetry collection, the best-selling *how to make a basket* (UQP, 2021) won the 2020 David Unaipon Award, and their second collection *mark the dawn* (UQP, 2024) was awarded the 2024 UQP Quentin Bryce Award. Jazz's first feature film *WINHANGANHA* (2023) interrogates the legacies of archives on First Nations people and was commissioned by the National Film and Sound Archive of Australia.

Sheila Ngọc Phạm is a writer, editor, producer, curator and researcher. She writes for literary and mainstream publications and has held editorial roles at the ABC, producing radio documentaries and stories. As an independent producer and curator, she has collaborated with cultural and artistic institutions, including the 2023 exhibition *MÌNH* for Fairfield City Museum and Gallery. Sheila recently completed her PhD at the Australian Institute of Health Innovation at Macquarie University and now works at the University of Sydney's Reproduction and Perinatal Centre based at Westmead Hospital. She is also the 2025 Imago Fellow at the State Library of New South Wales.

Professor Jakelin Troy is a researcher focused on documenting, describing and reviving indigenous languages, with a new focus on the indigenous languages of Pakistan, including Saraiki of the Punjab and Torwali of Swat. She is carrying out two Australian Research Council Discovery Projects, one (with Professor John Maynard) on the history of Aboriginal missions and reserves in eastern Australia, and the history of Aboriginal people who were not institutionalised. The other project is on the practice of 'corroboree' by Aboriginal people in the 'assimilation period' of the mid-twentieth century in Australia. Jaky is interested in the use of Indigenous research methodologies and community-engaged research practices. She is Aboriginal-Australian and her community is Ngarigu of the Snowy Mountains in south-eastern Australia.

Beth Yahp is a Senior Lecturer in Creative Writing at the University of Sydney. Her articles have been published in *a/b: Auto/Biography Studies*, *Life Writing* and *TEXT*, and her fiction and creative nonfiction include *The Red Pearl and Other Stories*; a memoir, *Eat First, Talk Later*, shortlisted for the 2018 Adelaide Festival Award for Literature (Non-Fiction); and a prize-winning novel, *The Crocodile Fury*. Beth wrote the libretto for composer Liza Lim's opera *Moon Spirit Feasting*, which won the APRA Award for Best Composition by an Australian Composer (2002). She developed and performed a season of performance-lectures as part of the Seymour Centre's *Art + Information* production, fusing poetry, drama and academia (2022). She is working, very slowly, on a series of *Small Pleasures*.

ACKNOWLEDGEMENTS

Thanks first to publisher Harriet McInerney, gentle and illuminating guide, for helping me to turn a pleasurable activity – walks with writers in a city of stories – into a book to be shared with readers.

To brilliant editor Emma Driver, I'm grateful for the cheerful fact-checking, comma wrangling and wise counsel. Thank you proofreader Anne Savage for your great care and graceful squiggles.

Thank you to everyone at NewSouth: Emma Hutchinson for expert steering of the craft, Joumana Awad for unstinting and cheerful support, Rosina Di Marzo for excellent work on publicity, and all the diligent and imaginative people who take NewSouth's beautiful books into the world.

For the beauty of this particular book: delighted thanks to cover designer and illustrator Mika Tabata and internal designer Josephine Pajor-Markus.

Thank you always and sincerely to Pippa Masson and all at Curtis Brown Australia, dauntless champions of Australian writing.

For project funding, thank you to Creative Australia, City of Sydney, Northern Beaches Council and the School of Art, Communication and English at the University of Sydney.

Thanks too to the University for making a home for my work, with particular gratitude to colleagues and students in the Discipline of English and Writing, who remind me continually of the joy of knowing our world and each other through language.

To filmmaker Kaye Harrison and composer Darcy Archer, thank you for the magical project film. Thank you Michael Daly for dazzling photography.

For an early taste of the adventure of exploring Sydney on foot, thank you Scott. For regular reminders of the expansive joys of walking and talking, thank you Lou.

To the writers who walked with me, thank you for showing me your Sydney with such warmth and generosity. I have continued to walk these places, with my feet and in my mind. This city forms a large part of my imaginative world; it is a true gift to have it so enriched.

Thank you finally to this blazing, dreamy city for the endless astonishment, and to Brad, Damien and Olive, for the happy home we've made here.

www.ingramcontent.com/pod-product-compliance
Lightning Source LLC
Chambersburg PA
CBHW030614230426
43661CB00053B/1986